the family table slow cooker

Easy, Healthy, and Delicious Recipes

Dominique DeVito

CHARTWELL
BOOKS

Inspiring | Educating | Creating | Entertaining

Brimming with creative inspiration, how-to projects, and useful information to enrich your everyday life, Quarto Knows is a favorite destination for those pursuing their interests and passions. Visit our site and dig deeper with our books into your area of interest: Quarto Creates, Quarto Cooks, Quarto Homes, Quarto Lives, Quarto Drives, Quarto Explores, Quarto Gifts, or Quarto Kids.

First published in 2018 by Chartwell Books,
an imprint of The Quarto Group
142 West 36th Street, 4th Floor
New York, NY 10018 USA
T (212) 779-4972 **F** (212) 779-6058
www.QuartoKnows.com

10 9 8 7 6 5 4 3 2 1

ISBN: 978-0-7858-3528-8

Food photography: Shutterstock

Location photography: Shutterstock, Warren Street Books, Zach Nevin

Cover and interior design: Corinda Cook

Packaging and design: Warren Street Books

Photo credits: All photos courtesy of Shutterstock © 2017. All Rights Reserved. Except for the following: Warren Street Books: p. 4, 26, 28 (middle, far left), 29 (bottom, far left), 58 (bottom, center), 59 (top, center and bottom, right), 96 (bottom, center), 97 (top, right and bottom, center), 122 (middle, center and bottom, middle), 144 (bottom, left), and 172 (top, right and bottom, right).

Printed in China

contents

introduction

Sitting down to dinner with your family is proven to be a beneficial experience for all of you. It's a time to reconnect, share, and appreciate what the day has brought you; a time to be nourished by the food and each other. Studies of school-age children whose families gather every night for dinner show better academic achievement, and they tend to lead healthier lives as they grow up, suffering less from obesity, diabetes, and other maladies.

But life is so hectic! Whether you live in the city, the suburbs, or the country, time is at a premium these days. There are so many demands —work, school, after-school activities, meetings, weekend events. All of this leaves little time to cook healthy, delicious meals.

The Family Table Slow Cooker can help change that. Slow cookers are engineered for you to be able to assemble simple ingredients and let the cooker do the work. You can choose locally grown fruits, vegetables, and herbs, locally raised meats, and local dairy products to prepare, or, if you don't have the time or budget for that, don't sweat it, frozen veggies and other grocery store selections can work, too! The idea is to get fantastic dishes onto the table for you and your family to share, and be able to share the events of the day well.

The Family Table Slow Cooker is a collection of easy-to-make, simple, and delicious family styled dishes from around the world. With more than seventy recipes (and over thirty variations),

this book offers a great assortment of amazing, tempting, outstanding healthy food choices that your family will ask for again and again. From classic french toast to roast chicken, to soups and stews, to risotto with asparagus, to roasts, shrimp scampi, Maryland styled crabs, savory artichokes, and even chocolate fondue! There's something for everyone to enjoy—especially the cook, who will be saving time and trouble. Perfect for the family dinner table, these crowd pleasing recipes are also perfect for family get togethers or dinner with friends.

Are you ready to make healthy, delicious meals that your whole family will love using simple ingredients that cook while you go do something else? Yes? Then this book is for you.

What kinds of meals and foods can you make in a slow cooker? The answer is limited only by your imagination and taste preferences. There are the classics, of course—beef stew, chili, soups of all kinds, and great mini meatballs. There are more exotic dishes like curried cauliflower or bouillabaisse or stewed figs. This book features one hundred twelve recipes that cover all the bases, from breakfast to finger foods to stews to desserts. It includes recipes steeped in American tradition, but also those with international flair, including escargots!

Don't let the slow cooker intimidate you. After you've made a few recipes, you'll get a feel for it. Every cook is different, and while they can all be using the same utensils, invariably they will do things slightly differently and produce different results. Trust your instincts with recipes you've traditionally made in the oven. For example, if you like to put beer in your chili, swap out another of the liquids in the recipe, or add some as an experiment. I tend to like things spicy, and you'll find recipes that include cayenne, hot pepper flakes, cumin, cinnamon, and so on. If those don't appeal to you, skip them or substitute with something you like.

Another consideration is the source of your ingredients. You'll maximize flavor and nutrition if you can choose locally grown fruits, vegetables, and herbs, locally raised meats, and local dairy products. But if you can't, don't sweat it. Fresh is best, of course, but it's great to be able to throw in a bag of frozen peas or broccoli florets. I buy the largest bag of frozen broccoli I can fit into my freezer in the winter because I like to put it in everything. The frozen pieces are so convenient. There are so many interesting combinations of frozen vegetables—and fruits—these days, that experimentation is becoming easier and more fun.

As for the care and keeping of your slow cooker, that's easy, too. Simply handle the insert with care, wash it with warm water and soap, dry it thoroughly, wipe down all surfaces of the outer part, and put it back together. Don't stash it too far out of reach, as you'll be less inclined to use it as frequently as it deserves to be used.

Most of all, take advantage of the time you can spend away from the stove and oven while your slow cooker is doing its thing, and trust that you'll come home to deliciousness. So reconnect with family and friends, gather and celebrate using these delicious recipes!

Happy Slow Cooking!

Meet the Inventor

The inventor of the slow cooker as we know it was Irving Naxon. In 1936, at age thirty-four, he applied for a patent for a device that could heat foods in an insert that was surrounded by a heating device. After several mutations, he patented the Naxon Beanery in 1940. He would also call it the Boston Beanery, and the Flavor Crock. Naxon was an engineer and inventor with over two hundred patents in his name, including the Zipper in Times Square that wraps around buildings and shows news headlines. Naxon died in 1989, but the Crock Pot (slow cooker) lives on. There's even one in the Smithsonian Museum!

breakfast
treats

cinnamon bread pudding

Who doesn't like cinnamon-raisin bread? Is there anything more fragrant than the smell of cinnamon-raisin bread baking or cooking in the kitchen? It fills you up with warmth and a smile. A great way to start off your morning!

Nonstick cooking spray

8 slices cinnamon-raisin bread, cut or broken into large pieces (about 5 cups, or 175 g)

1 14-ounce (400 g) can sweetened condensed milk

1 cup (235 ml) water

1 teaspoon vanilla extract

½ teaspoon cinnamon

4 eggs, beaten

Dollop yogurt or crème fraiche, for serving

1. Spray the inside of the slow cooker with nonstick cooking spray.

2. Place the bread pieces inside.

3. Combine the milk, water, vanilla extract, and eggs, and pour over the chunks of bread, gently stirring with a wooden spoon to coat the bread with the milk mixture.

4. Cook on Low for 2½ to 3 hours.

5. Serve warm with a dollop of yogurt or crème fraiche.

This is definitely a breakfast for those with a sweet tooth! If you want to reduce the sweetness, you can substitute a thick bread like challah or a thick-cut white bread for the cinnamon-raisin bread. You can also add ½ cup (75 g) of dried currants or raisins for added flavor and texture.

banana oatmeal

There's something about bananas that makes hot cereals especially tasty. Slow cooking them with the oatmeal intensifies the flavors.

makes 6 servings

4 cups (1 L) water

1 cup (160 g) steel-cut oats

½ cup (110 g) dark brown sugar, plus extra for topping

¼ teaspoon salt

2 to 3 ripe bananas, peeled and mashed

Sliced bananas, for topping

1. In a large bowl, combine the water, oats, brown sugar, salt, and mashed bananas together, then pour into the slow cooker.

2. Cook on Low for 6 hours. Stir before serving.

3. Top servings with slices of banana and additional brown sugar, if desired.

oatmeal with pumpkin

Use canned pureed pumpkin in this recipe, not the canned pumpkin that has pie spices in it. Pumpkin is nutritious and delicious, and adds a nice earthy color to this dish.

makes 6 servings

6 cups (1.5 L) water

1 15-ounce (425 g) can pumpkin puree

1½ cups (240 g) steel-cut oats

½ cup (110 g) brown sugar

1 teaspoon ground cinnamon

½ teaspoon ground nutmeg

1. In a large bowl, combine the water, pumpkin puree, oats, brown sugar, cinnamon, and nutmeg.

2. Pour the mixture gently into the slow cooker.

3. Cook on Low for 6 hours. Stir before serving.

egg, cheese, and sausage casserole

Here's an easy breakfast casserole to throw together and enjoy later, preferably the next morning. You can also use pork sausage, but I prefer a leaner turkey sausage. Experiment with the proportions of the cheeses, too, or if you don't want something spicy, choose a mozzarella or load up on the Cheddar.

makes 8 servings

½ pound (227 g)
turkey sausage

Nonstick cooking spray

10 slices sandwich bread
(whole grain is best),
cut or broken into cubes,
or about 6 cups (750 g)

1 cup (120 g) grated
Cheddar cheese

1½ cups (180 g) grated
Monterey Jack cheese

12 eggs

2¼ cups (540 ml) milk

1 teaspoon salt

½ teaspoon freshly ground
black pepper

1 teaspoon ground sage

1. In a skillet over medium heat, brown the turkey sausage until cooked through, about 10 minutes. Drain thoroughly to remove as much fat as possible. Spray the inside of the slow cooker with the cooking spray.

2. Make the casserole by starting with a layer of bread cubes, topping with sausage, and then sprinkling both cheeses over the top.

3. Continue layering bread, sausage, and cheese until ingredients are used up (approximately 3 layers).

4. In a large bowl, whisk the eggs, then add the milk, salt, pepper, and sage, stirring to combine. Pour the egg mixture over the layers in the slow cooker.

5. Cover and cook on Low for about 8 hours. It's done when a knife inserted in the middle comes out clean.

broccoli-red pepper frittata

If you're someone who enjoys veggies with your eggs, this is a great go-to baked-egg dish. The broccoli—along with the red pepper—add color, flavor, and vitamins.

makes 6 servings

2 tablespoons olive oil

1 medium onion, chopped

2 cloves garlic, minced

½ red bell pepper, seeds and ribs removed, cut into dime-size pieces

8 large eggs

3 tablespoons low-fat milk

¾ cup (130 g) fresh broccoli florets, cut into bite-size pieces

¼ cup (20 g) Parmesan cheese

2 tablespoons fresh chopped parsley

1 tablespoon fresh thyme, chopped

Salt and pepper, to taste

1. Heat the olive oil in a skillet and add the onion, garlic, and red bell pepper. Cook over medium-high heat until the onion is translucent, about 3 minutes.

2. In a large bowl, whisk the eggs with the milk. Stir in the broccoli, Parmesan, and herbs. Stir in the onion/garlic/red pepper mix. Season with the salt and pepper.

3. Take a large piece of heavy-duty aluminum foil and place it in the slow cooker so it comes up the sides of the cooker. It's fine if the foil extends over the sides. Pour the egg mixture gently into the slow cooker on top of the foil. Cover and cook on Low for 6 to 8 hours or on High for 2 to 2½ hours, or until eggs are set.

4. Run a spatula along the sides of the cooker to loosen the foil. Lift the frittata out of the slow cooker with the foil, and slide the cooked eggs onto a serving plate.

banana bread

Sure you can make banana bread in the oven, but it's equally successful in the slow cooker. The loaf will be a funny shape, but it'll taste good. Have fun with this one!

makes 6 servings

5 eggs, beaten

3 ½ cups (820 ml) low-fat milk

2 teaspoons vanilla

1 tablespoon ground cinnamon

½ teaspoon salt

6 cups (750 g) plain bread crumbs (or more to make mixture as thick as cooked oatmeal when mixed with all ingredients)

¾ cup (170 g) packed brown sugar

1 tablespoon butter, melted

3 ripe bananas, mashed or sliced

Nonstick cooking spray

1. In a large bowl, combine all the ingredients together until the bread crumbs are thoroughly wet, and the mixture is smooth, like thick oatmeal.

2. Spray the slow cooker with the nonstick cooking spray and transfer the mixture into it. Cover and cook on Low for 6 to 8 hours or on High for 4 to 5 hours.

3. When cooked, a knife stuck in the middle will come out fairly clean. Serve warm.

IMPORTANT! For the last half hour of cooking, prop the lid open with a spoon. This will allow the moisture to escape. If you don't do this, you will have a layer of liquid around the banana bread.

egg bake with spinach and mushrooms

Nutritious, delicious, and a great start to a busy day! You could add cheese to this dish to give it flavor and substance, but it's quite tasty without it, and you won't be weighed down by the cheese as you start your day.

makes 6 servings

Nonstick cooking spray

2 tablespoons olive oil

½ onion, finely chopped

1 cup (70 g) sliced domestic mushrooms

4 cups (120 g) fresh spinach leaves, coarse stems removed, and ripped or cut into smaller pieces

12 eggs

¾ cup (180 ml) half-and-half

1 cup (115 g) shredded mozzarella cheese (optional)

1 tablespoon chopped fresh parsley

Salt and pepper, to taste

1. Lightly grease the inside of the slow cooker with the nonstick cooking spray.

2. In large skillet, heat the olive oil over medium heat. Cook the onion and mushrooms until tender, about 5 minutes.

3. Turn the heat off, place the spinach leaves over the onions and mushrooms, and cover with a tight-fitting lid. Allow the spinach to steam under the lid for about 10 minutes, which will cause it to wilt.

4. In a large bowl, beat the eggs with the half-and-half until well combined. Add the onion, mushroom, and spinach mixture, and stir in the cheese, if desired. Add the parsley, season with the salt and pepper, and stir just to combine.

5. Pour the mixture into the slow cooker, cover, and cook on Low for about 4 to 6 hours, until eggs are thoroughly cooked. When cooled, insert a knife in the center. If it comes out clean, the dish is ready.

This is delicious served with a fresh salsa. Chop 2 very ripe tomatoes and put them in a small bowl. Add a squirt of lime juice, a tablespoon of finely minced onion, a clove of crushed garlic, and a teaspoon or so of chopped jalapeño pepper (or other spicy pepper of your choice). Season with pepper and just a dash of salt.

garden vegetable eggs

Besides making a wonderful breakfast, this colorful egg dish can also be served as a light lunch or dinner with a big salad—using some of the same vegetables!

makes 6 to 8 servings

2 tablespoons plus ¼ cup (60 ml) olive oil

1 onion, finely chopped

2 cloves garlic, minced

1 small zucchini, cubed

1 small green bell pepper, seeded and cubed

2 ripe plum tomatoes, roughly chopped

8 eggs

½ cup (120 ml) water

Salt and pepper, to taste

¼ cup (10 g) chopped fresh basil

1. Lightly grease the inside of the slow cooker with the olive oil.

2. In a large skillet over medium heat, warm the remaining oil and add the onion and garlic. Stir, cooking, until the onion is translucent, about 3 minutes.

3. Add the zucchini and green bell pepper and continue to stir while cooking until just tender, about 5 minutes.

4. Add the tomatoes, stir, and remove from heat, stir for 2 minutes.

5. In a large bowl, beat the eggs with the water until well mixed. Add the vegetable mixture, and stir until just combined. Season with the salt and pepper.

6. Pour the eggs and vegetables into the slow cooker, cover, and cook on Low for 4 to 6 hours, until the eggs are thoroughly cooked.

7. Add the basil in the last half hour of cooking. When done, insert a clean knife in the center. If it comes out clean, the dish is ready.

crustless mushroom and onion quiche

This is a delicious mushroom and onion concoction that's rich with tangy earth flavors and sweet, caramelized onions. The cheese is essential to the overall flavor and texture of the dish.

makes 4 to 6 servings

¼ cup or ½ stick (60 g) salted butter

½ cup (80 g) Vidalia onion, sliced into ribbons

2 cups (140 g) sliced fresh mushrooms (this can be any kind or combination of mushrooms from domestic to portobello, cremini, shiitake etc.)

½ teaspoon dried sage

Salt and pepper, to taste

10 eggs

1 cup (250 ml) half-and-half

1 cup (110 g) shredded Swiss cheese

1 tablespoon each chopped fresh dill and chives, for garnish

1. In a skillet over medium-high heat, melt the butter. Add the onions and stir until wilted, about 2 minutes. Add the mushroom slices and cook, stirring, until they start to soften and shrink, about 5 minutes. Remove from heat.

2. Drain any liquid produced by the mushrooms. Stir in the sage, and season with the salt and pepper.

3. In a bowl, beat the eggs. Add the half-and-half and the cheese, and then add the mushroom and onion mix.

4. Transfer everything to the slow cooker, cover, and cook on Low for 4 to 6 hours, until a knife inserted in the center comes out clean. Be careful not to overcook. Serve hot. Garnish with chopped dill and chives, if desired.

If you want to add meat to this recipe, sauté some bacon until crumbly. Add it to the mushroom mixture before cooking, or sprinkle it on top at the end.

crustless spinach quiche

Who says you need a doughy crust to make a good pie? This one is great for a summer brunch and features sun-dried tomatoes and fresh herbs for a fresh and fabulous taste.

makes 2 to 4 servings

10 eggs

2 tablespoons half-and-half

½ teaspoon salt

¼ teaspoon freshly ground pepper

¼ teaspoon cayenne pepper

¼ cup (32 g) oil-packed sun-dried tomatoes, blotted dry

1 tablespoon fresh basil, chopped

4 cups (120 g) fresh baby spinach, coarsely chopped

1. In a large bowl, whisk together the eggs, half-and-half, salt, pepper, and cayenne.

2. Place the tomatoes at the bottom of the slow cooker, arranging them so that they touch but don't overlap, forming a "crust." Sprinkle the basil over the tomatoes.

3. Pour the egg mixture over the tomatoes and place the spinach leaves on top. Cover and cook on Low for 4 hours or on High for 2 to 3 hours, until the eggs are set. Test for doneness by inserting a knife in the center. It should come out clean.

You could substitute dried mushrooms for the tomatoes, or create a combination with both of them. The idea is to have a firm and chewy base of vegetables.

hearty and hot almond meal

This is a great gluten-free "porridge" that's perfect for cold winter mornings or for before or after intense workouts. Add dried fruits such as cranberries, currants, or raisins. You can cook them with the cereal or sprinkle them on top when the cereal is cooked.

makes 4 to 6 servings

1 firm baking apple, like Granny Smith or Empire apple, peeled and chopped

1 Anjou or Bosc pear, cored and chopped

4 cups (500 g) almond meal

4 cups (1 L) water

Dash salt

½ teaspoon cinnamon

½ teaspoon nutmeg

1. Place the chopped fruit in the bottom of the slow cooker.

2. Cover with the almond meal. Add the water and salt. Stir to combine.

3. Cover and cook on Low for 5 to 6 hours, until all water is absorbed and the fruit is tender.

appetizers and finger foods

sausage and pancetta wraps

When these moist and meaty treats are cooked through, cut them into slices and serve with toothpicks for easy eating. Depending on the kind of sausage you choose, the dish can take on a range of tastes. Serve with mustard or a dipping sauce.

makes 10 to 12 servings

2 pounds (1 kg) Italian sausage links

1 pound (454 g) pancetta, sliced thick

Honey, to drizzle

1. Work with whole sausage links and individual slices of pancetta. Lay the pancetta down on a plate or piece of wax paper, place the sausage at one end, and wrap the pancetta around the sausage, working at an angle so the pancetta covers the entire link. Secure the ends with wooden toothpicks.

2. Place the wrapped sausages in the slow cooker and drizzle lightly with honey. Stack in layers until all the sausages are in the slow cooker.

3. Cover and cook on Low for 4 to 6 hours or on High for about 3 hours. Remove with tongs, slice into bite-size pieces, and put a toothpick into every piece to secure the pancetta and make for easy eating.

While choosing Italian sausages is easiest—and these are available in either sweet or hot varieties—you can experiment with all different kinds of sausage. Try this recipe with seasoned chicken sausage, for example, or with pieces of kielbasa. The only kind of sausage links to avoid are those made for breakfast, as they are too small.

seasoned mini meatballs

For whatever reason, meatballs are a happy food (like cupcakes). There's something fun about them. This recipe features meatballs that are seasoned with parsley, garlic, thyme, and fennel—a delicious combination. They are yummy on their own or with a sauce.

makes about 24 small meatballs

2 pounds (1 kg) ground beef

2 teaspoons fresh thyme, finely chopped

1 teaspoon ground fennel seeds

2 tablespoons fresh parsley, minced

1 large egg, beaten

¼ onion, finely minced

2 cloves garlic, minced

3 tablespoons olive oil

Salt and pepper, to taste

1. In a large bowl, combine the ground beef, thyme, fennel seeds, parsley, egg, onion, and garlic. Stir to combine well.

2. Form the meat mixture into meatballs and set aside on a plate.

3. In a large skillet, heat olive oil over medium-high heat. Add the meatballs (in batches if necessary) and turn them so they brown on all sides.

4. Using a slotted spoon, transfer the browned meatballs to the slow cooker.

5. Cover and cook on Low for 3 to 4 hours, or on High for 2 to 3 hours.

6. Season with the salt and pepper.

These meatballs are delicious on their own, but are sensational with dipping sauces. A classic Italian marinara (tomato sauce) is wonderful, as is something less traditional, like a horse-radish sauce. Make a simple one by combining ¼ cup fresh grated horseradish with 1 cup of Greek yogurt, 1 Tablespoon Dijon mustard, 1 teaspoon fresh lemon juice, and salt and pepper to taste.

cauliflower italiano

Cauliflower is a vegetable that is meaty and substantial and can therefore be cooked in a number of ways—whole, in pieces, even chopped or grated. In this recipe, the florets cook with an Italian herb blend and the result is a finger food that's delicious and nutritious!

makes about 6 servings

1 large head of cauliflower

¼ cup (60 ml) olive oil

Freshly ground black pepper

1½ teaspoons sea salt

2 cloves minced garlic

1 tablespoon minced fresh oregano or 1 teaspoon dried oregano

1 tablespoon minced fresh parsley or 1 teaspoon dried parsley

Lemon slices for garnish, if desired

1. Core the cauliflower and break the head up into florets. You can trim and cut the stems into bite-size pieces, as well.

2. Put the pieces into the slow cooker. Drizzle with olive oil so that there is a light coating on the cauliflower. Season the oiled cauliflower with the pepper and salt, add the garlic, and stir.

3. Cover and cook on Low for 4 hours, or on High for 2 hours. Sprinkle the cauliflower with the herbs, just so the florets and stems are covered and stir. Put the cover back on and continue to cook for another 30 minutes until the cauliflower is tender.

4. Serve in a bowl with long toothpicks. Add lemon slices for garnish, if desired.

For a more colorful dish, replace half of the head of cauliflower with half a head of broccoli.

simple poached shrimp

Use the slow cooker to poach the shrimp, and then stir the warm seafood in the oil and lemon mixture. Close your eyes and imagine yourself on the Adriatic coast of Italy. You've arrived!

makes 4 to 6 servings

8 cups (2 L) water

¼ bulb fennel, leaves removed and cut into thick strips

1 small carrot, peeled

1 tablespoon white wine vinegar

½ cup (120 ml) freshly squeezed lemon juice

½ cup (120 ml) extra virgin olive oil (the fruitier the better)

2 pounds (1 kg) small, fresh shrimp, uncooked, shells on

1 teaspoon fresh parsley, minced

Salt and pepper, to taste

1. Put the water, fennel, carrot, and vinegar in the slow cooker. If you plan to serve the shrimp sooner rather than later, turn the cooker on High and let the vegetables poach for about 3 hours. If you want to do this while you're out for the day, put the cooker on Low and leave it for 6 to 8 hours. The water should be very hot—if it was on the stove, it would be close to boiling.

2. While the vegetables are poaching, prepare the lemon and oil. Combine them in a medium-size bowl and stir with a whisk. Set aside.

3. When the water in the slow cooker is very hot, remove and discard the poached vegetables and add the shrimp.

4. Cover and cook on High for 10 to 30 minutes. Check after 10 minutes, and every 5 minutes thereafter. Cooking time will depend on the size of the shrimp. When cooked, the shrimp will turn pink and firm but not hard. It's important not to overcook them.

5. When cooked, drain the shrimp and peel them, placing the warm, peeled shrimp in the bowl with the oil and lemon mixture. When all the shrimp have been added, stir, sprinkle with parsley, season with the salt and pepper, and serve immediately.

A slow cooker is not meant to boil things. That's one of the great things about it and why you don't have to worry about leaving it on all day. When it comes to a recipe like this, where you want to cook something quickly in a hot liquid, you need to factor in the time it's going to take for the broth to get very hot. Another benefit to this method is that you have more flexibility with the cooking time of the shrimp, and don't have to worry about them rapidly overcooking.

portobellos with rosemary

A juicy slice of portobello mushroom cooked in butter and oil with fresh herbs is, simply, fabulously delicious. Letting the mushrooms slow-cook is a way to achieve perfection. Enjoy!

makes about 4 servings

3 large portobello
mushrooms, loose

3 tablespoons olive oil

3 tablespoons salted butter

Salt and pepper, to taste

1 tablespoon chopped
fresh rosemary

1. Go over the portobellos and remove any obvious dirt by brushing or shaking. Slice the portobellos into thick slices (approximately ¼-inch or 6 mm). Put the slices into the slow cooker.

2. In a small skillet, heat the olive oil and butter over low heat until melted and combined. Pour the combination over the mushrooms.

3. Cover and cook on Low for 3 to 4 hours or on High for 1 to 2 hours. The mushrooms should be cooked through but not mushy. Season lightly with the salt and pepper and sprinkle with fresh rosemary before serving.

The portobello mushroom is an oversized cremini mushroom. Both are dark brown mushrooms related to the common mushroom. Creminis and portobellos share a mustier, earthier flavor as well as color from the common white mushroom. Large portobellos are so meaty that they are often cooked as meat substitutes, making great "burgers" for vegetarians. Roasted peppers are a lovely accompaniment with large portobello mushrooms.

lamb kabobs

You'll be eager to eat these when you smell them cooking. This is a recipe full of Mediterranean goodness. Lamb is eaten much more around the world than in the US, where beef is "king."

makes 6 to 10 kabobs

½ cup (120 ml) olive oil

1 teaspoon rosemary, minced

3 cloves garlic, minced

¼ teaspoon salt

¼ teaspoon pepper

1 pound (454 g) boneless leg of lamb, cubed

2 red bell peppers, cored, seeded, and cut into chunks

1 onion, peeled and cut into small wedges

1 large zucchini, cut into thick slices

Wooden skewer sticks, broken to fit the length of the slow cooker

1. In a large bowl, combine the olive oil, rosemary, garlic, and salt and pepper. Add the lamb cubes and stir to coat.

2. Using wooden skewers, make kabobs alternating lamb, red bell peppers, onions, and zucchini.

3. Lay the kabobs in the slow cooker, and pour the remaining oil mixture from the large bowl over them.

4. Cover and cook on Low for 3 to 4 hours or on High for 1 to 2 hours until lamb is cooked through and vegetables have softened. Baste with juices from the slow cooker before serving.

These are delicious dipped in dipped in mint sauce or mint jelly, which you can purchase at the grocery store. You can also "sandwich" a kabob in a lettuce leaf and top with some baba ghanoush (See recipe on page 46).

braised baby artichokes with prosciutto

Baby artichokes, like soft-shelled crabs, are entirely edible—you don't have to remove the hairy "choke." Just slice, cook, and eat!

makes 6 to 8 servings

6 cups (1.5 L) cold water

2 lemons, halved

24 baby artichokes

3 tablespoons olive oil

3 shallots, diced

2 cloves garlic, minced

1 cup (125 g) prosciutto, chopped

¼ cup (60 ml) chicken stock or broth

½ cup (120 ml) dry white wine

2 tablespoons freshly squeezed lemon juice (seeds removed)

½ teaspoon dried thyme

1 bay leaf

Salt and pepper, to taste

Fresh chopped parsley, for garnish

1. Place water in a large mixing bowl, with freshly squeezed lemon juice and lemon halves.

2. Work on one artichoke at a time because they discolor very quickly. If there is a stem, trim and peel the dark green skin from the stem. Break off all the small, dark leaves from the bottom so that the artichoke resembles a rose bud. Cut off the top 1 inch (2.5 cm), and then cut them in half lengthwise. Place in the lemon water, and repeat until all artichokes are trimmed.

3. Heat oil in a large skillet over medium-high heat. Add the shallots, garlic, and prosciutto, and cook, stirring frequently, for 3 minutes, or until shallots are translucent. Drain artichokes and add them to the skillet along with stock, wine, lemon juice, thyme, and bay leaf. Bring to a boil, and then transfer mixture to the slow cooker.

4. Cook on Low for 3 to 4 hours or on High for 1½ to 2 hours, or until artichokes are very tender.

5. Remove and discard bay leaf. Season with the salt and pepper. Sprinkle with fresh parsley when serving.

Toasted pine nuts are an excellent complement to this dish, as they add a buttery crunchiness to it, and the flavors pair perfectly. To toast the pine nuts, put them in a heavy clad or nonstick skillet and heat them over medium heat. Stir with a wooden spoon while they heat, taking care not to overdo them. The process takes 3 to 5 minutes.

stuffed mushrooms

Stuffed mushrooms are typically cooked in an oven and a crispy breadcrumb topping. Done in a slow cooker, these turn out softer and more succulent. If you want them crispier, place them on a cookie shoot and broil them slightly. The texture and taste will already be there. The liquid produced by the cooked mushrooms is great to add to soup or stew.

makes 4 to 6 servings

1 pound (454 g) large white mushrooms

½ cup (64 g) chopped portobello mushroom

¼ pound (113 g) pancetta or thick-cut bacon, finely chopped

4 fresh anchovy fillets, minced

2 cloves garlic, pressed

1 egg

3 tablespoons fresh parsley, chopped

Salt and pepper, to taste

¼ cup (32 g) almond meal

¼ cup (32 g) golden flax meal

1 teaspoon cornstarch

Olive oil, for drizzling

1. Clean the white mushrooms to be stuffed by dabbing at them to remove any dirt with a wet paper towel. If the mushrooms have stems, gently remove them. When cleaned, place them cap side down in the slow cooker.

2. In a large mixing bowl, combine the chopped portobello mushroom, pancetta, anchovies, garlic, egg, and parsley. Stir with a fork to combine, further mashing it into a somewhat fine-textured mix. Season with the salt and pepper.

3. Spoon the mixture evenly into all the mushroom caps.

4. In a small bowl, combine the almond and flax meals and the cornstarch. Sprinkle this liberally over the stuffed mushrooms. Drizzle with some olive oil.

5. Cook on Low for 4 to 6 Hours or on High for 3 hours, until the mushrooms are tender and the filling is cooked. Remove the stuffed mushrooms carefully and either serve immediately or place under the broiler for 2 to 4 minutes, if desired.

baba ghanoush

This is an eggplant dip that also makes a great spread on large lettuce leaves when making wraps of any kind. Or you could do what I do, which is just eat it by the spoonful!

makes about 4 servings

1 large eggplant

1 tablespoon olive oil

4 cloves garlic, chopped

2 tablespoons tahini
(raw, not roasted)

2 tablespoons fresh-squeezed
lemon juice

1 teaspoon tomato paste

1 teaspoon salt

¼ teaspoon pepper

¼ teaspoon cayenne (optional)

1. Cut the very top off of the eggplant. Slice it into quarters, and peel the skin off with a paring knife.

2. In a bowl, combine the olive oil, garlic, tahini, lemon juice, tomato paste, salt, pepper, and cayenne.

3. Place the eggplant in the slow cooker and pour the oil mix over it. Cover and cook on Low for 5 to 6 hours. Mash with a fork before serving.

Tahini is a paste made from sesame seeds. Find a raw tahini in your health food store, if possible, and buy only a small quantity. It's the processing of the seeds for commercial tahinis that can tarnish the nutritive value of the paste.

devils on horseback

Here's a slow-cooker take on the classic cocktail party food of the 1970s. Be sure to crack the lid on the slow cooker as directed so the bacon gets a bit crispy.

makes 24 servings

24 large dates, pitted

12 slices thick-cut bacon, halved

1. Wrap each date in a piece of bacon and secure with a toothpick.

2. Place the "devils" in the slow cooker. Their sides can touch. Cover and cook on Low for about 5 hours, or on High for about 3 hours.

3. During the last hour, prop the lid open with the handle of a wooden spoon. This allows the steam to escape and makes the bacon crispier. Serve hot.

If you want an extra layer of flavor, consider drizzling the wraps with a tiny bit of honey— just enough for a drop or two per wrap. You can also sprinkle them lightly with cayenne or curry powder during the last hour of cooking when the lid is ajar for an extra zing.

curried cauliflower

Really easy to make, and really tasty! Vary the amounts of the spices if you lean more toward the flavor of one over another.

1 head cauliflower

Olive oil, for drizzling

½ teaspoon ground cumin

½ teaspoon ground turmeric

½ teaspoon ground cayenne

½ teaspoon ground coriander

1. Core the cauliflower and break the head up into florets. You can trim and cut the stems into bite-size pieces, as well.

2. Put the pieces into the slow cooker. Drizzle with olive oil so that there is a light coating of oil on the cauliflower. Lightly dust the oiled cauliflower with the spices, just so the florets and stems are covered. If you are a hesitant cook who isn't sure about quantities, you can combine about ¼ cup (60 ml) olive oil with 2 teaspoons curry powder—which is a pre-combined blend of the spices listed above—and pour this over the cauliflower.

3. Cover and cook on Low for 4 to 5 hours, or on High for 2 to 3 hours until the cauliflower is tender. Serve in a bowl with long toothpicks.

For a more colorful dish, replace half of the head of cauliflower with half a head of broccoli, or one cubed potato, or two or three sliced carrots, or one small can of peas. To add more color and flavor try adding one red bell pepper sliced. Another idea might be to add one small can of tomato sauce for an extra flavor.

spiced pistachios

Raw pistachios are a great source of thiamine, Vitamin B6, copper, and manganese. Originating in Iran and Iraq, pistachios are now grown around the world, including in California.

makes 4 cups (1 L)

2 tablespoons coconut oil

¼ cup (85 g) honey

1 teaspoon ground ginger

1 teaspoon ground cumin

½ teaspoon cayenne pepper

¼ teaspoon onion powder

¼ teaspoon garlic powder

4 cups (500 g) raw pistachios, unshelled

1. In a large skillet over medium heat, add the coconut oil. When it is melted, turn off the heat and add the honey, ginger, cumin, cayenne, onion powder, and garlic powder. When all are combined, stir in the nuts and continue stirring to coat them with the seasonings.

2. Scrape nuts into the slow cooker. Cover and cook on High for about 1 hour. Open and stir the nuts, then cover and continue cooking on High another 40 to 60 minutes.

3. Take the lid off the slow cooker and cook an additional 30 minutes or so until the nuts are dry.

4. Remove and allow to cool before storing in airtight containers.

Make curried pistachios by substituting 2 teaspoons of curry powder for the ginger and cumin. Keep the cayenne if you like some heat. You can omit the onion and garlic powders, too.

mustard and garlic drumsticks

The dry mustard and garlic combine to make a zesty and flavorful "rub" that slow-cooks the drumsticks to perfection.

makes 4 to 6 servings

3 pounds (1.3 kg) chicken legs (drumsticks)

¼ cup (85 g) honey

¼ cup or ½ stick (60 g) butter, melted

2 tablespoons dry mustard

½ teaspoon cayenne

3 cloves garlic, minced

Salt and pepper, to taste

1. Preheat the oven to 400°F (200°C). Line a cookie sheet with parchment paper and put the drumsticks on it. Cook for about 4 minutes, flip the chicken, and cook for an additional 4 minutes. Remove from the oven.

2. Place drumsticks in the slow cooker.

3. In a small bowl, combine the honey, melted butter, mustard, cayenne, and garlic. Stir to combine, and pour over the drumsticks. Stir the drumsticks so the sauce thoroughly covers them.

4. Cover and cook on Low for 4 to 5 hours or on High for 2 to 3 hours. Before serving, season with the salt and pepper.

Mustard is a fascinating and ancient plant with many benefits. It grows quickly and easily in the right zone, and produces beautiful yellow flowers on tall stems. Nearly all parts of the mustard plant are edible, too. The seeds are what's used to produce the condiment we know and love, but you can use the leaves and flowers in salads, to sauté in some oil with garlic, or as an addition to soups and stews.

escargot "magnifique"

Like fish, snails are high in protein and low in fat. Considered a delicacy in many parts of the world, and best known as the French preparation, escargot—prepared in butter, garlic, and parsley make a very tasty slow-cooked snack.

makes 4 servings

2 7.75-ounce (220 g) cans
Roland large snails
(24 snails total)

¼ cup or ½ stick (60 g)
unsalted butter

4 cloves garlic, crushed
in a garlic press

2 tablespoons fresh
parsley, chopped

Salt and pepper, to taste

1. Drain and rinse the snails. In a skillet over medium heat, melt the butter. Add the garlic, stirring til fragrant, about 2 minutes.

2. Add the snails and continue to cook until coated with the garlic butter, about 2 minutes.

3. Add the parsley, remove from the heat, stir, and transfer to the slow cooker. Cook on High for about 1 hour until heated through.

4. Season with the salt and pepper. Serve with toothpicks and a side dish of the garlic sauce, or wrap a few in a lettuce leaf.

If you want to pretend you're in a French cooking class, while the snails are still hot in the slow cooker, pour in ¼ cup (60 ml) vermouth. Shake to distribute, then light a match over the cooker to light the alcohol on fire. It will burn for just a minute, leaving behind the flavor.

soups, stews, and chilis

super-simple split pea soup

There's nothing like a thick pea soup on a cold night, and when you put this one together in the morning, you'll be delighted with the result later in the day. The soup tastes even better the next day!

makes 6 servings

1 16-ounce (454 g) bag green split peas

1 tablespoon salted butter

1 small onion, diced

1 clove garlic, minced

1 large potato, peeled and cubed (Idaho or Russet)

4 carrots, peeled and cut into ¼-inch (6 mm) slices

1 celery stalk, cleaned and diced, or ½ teaspoon celery seed

4 cups (1 L) vegetable or chicken broth

4 cups (1 L) water

Salt and pepper, to taste

1. To prepare, put peas into a colander and pick through them to remove any overly dark or dirty ones. Rinse with cold water and shake dry.

2. In a skillet over medium heat, melt the butter. Add the onions and garlic and cook, stirring, until the onion is softened, about 5 minutes. Remove from the heat and stir in the damp peas.

3. Add peas, potato, carrot, and celery into the slow cooker, and cover with broth and water. Cook on Low for 8 to 10 hours until peas are soft. Stir. Puree if desired. Season with the salt and pepper.

A great twist on this is to garnish with some freshly cooked crisp bacon.

chickpea soup
with hearty greens

Chickpeas are not only delicious but full of nutrients, including protein, fiber, manganese, and folate. The cumin adds a rich fragrance and warm spice. Take the time to soak dried chickpeas overnight—that's how you'll get the most flavor and nutritional value.

makes 8 servings

1 pound (454 g) dried chickpeas

1 cup (250 ml) water

6 cups (1.5 L) beef broth

2 bay leaves

1 tablespoon salted butter

1 large onion, chopped

3 garlic cloves, minced

1 teaspoon cumin

1 large head escarole, kale, or Swiss chard, chopped, washed, and dried

Salt and pepper, to taste

1. Soak the chickpeas overnight in enough water to cover them. Drain and rinse.

2. Put the drained beans in the slow cooker. Add the water, beef broth and bay leaves.

3. In a skillet over medium heat, melt the butter, cook the onion and garlic and then for about 5 minutes. Stir in the cumin.

4. Add the cooked onion/garlic mix to the slow cooker and stir in the chickpeas and liquids. Cover and cook on Low for 8 hours or on High for 3 to 4 hours or until chickpeas are tender.

5. When the chickpeas are thoroughly cooked, add the chopped greens. Season with the salt and pepper. Stir and recover, cooking another 20 to 30 minutes on Low. Stir and serve.

vegetable soup with herb oil

What makes this soup so special is the contrast between the mellow, long-simmered flavors of the soup and the freshness of the herb oil.

makes 6 servings

SOUP

3 tablespoons olive oil

1 medium yellow onion, diced

3 cloves garlic, minced

2 stalks of chopped celery

2 large carrots, peeled and sliced

½ fennel bulb, cored and sliced, fronds discarded

2 cups (140 g) thinly sliced green cabbage, firmly packed

1 medium zucchini, diced

1 medium yellow squash, diced

5 cups (1.3 L) vegetable stock

1 bay leaf

2 tablespoons chopped fresh parsley

1 teaspoon dried oregano

1 tablespoon fresh thyme

1 15-ounce (425 g) can garbanzo beans, drained and rinsed

¼ pound (225 g) whole grain pasta shells, cooked according to package until al dente

Salt and pepper, to taste

HERB OIL

¾ cup (45 g) firmly packed parsley leaves

1 clove garlic, minced

2 tablespoons chopped fresh basil

1 tablespoon chopped fresh rosemary

½ cup (120 ml) olive oil

Salt and pepper, to taste

1. Make the soup. Heat oil in a large stockpot over medium-high heat. Add onion, garlic, celery, carrots, fennel and cabbage. Cook, stirring frequently, for about 8 minutes, or until onion is translucent and cabbage is softened.

2. Remove from the heat and stir in the zucchini and yellow squash. Scrape mixture into the slow cooker.

3. Add stock, bay leaf, parsley, oregano, and thyme, and stir all ingredients together. Cover and cook on Low for 6 to 8 hours or on High for 3 to 4 hours, or until vegetables are tender.

4. Add garbanzo beans to the slow cooker and cook for another 30 to 45 minutes, on High until simmering. Remove and discard bay leaf, add pasta, and season with the salt and pepper.

5. While soup simmers, prepare herb oil by combining parsley, garlic, basil, rosemary, and olive oil in a food processor or blender. Puree until smooth, season with the salt and pepper, and scrape mixture into a bowl. To serve, ladle hot soup into bowls and drizzle some herb oil on top.

cabbage-carrot soup

Cabbage has an almost pungent taste, while carrots are naturally sweet. Combining these two—with an apple and zucchini to boot—makes for a soup with a lot of layered flavors.

makes 6 servings

¼ cup or ½ stick (60 g) unsalted butter

1 large onion, chopped

1 pound (454 g) green cabbage, washed and sliced thin

2 small zucchini, washed and sliced thin

2 carrots, peeled and sliced thin

1 Fuji apple, peeled and sliced thin

4 cups (1 L) chicken broth

½ cup (120 ml) dry white wine

Salt and pepper, to taste

1. Heat the butter in a skillet and add the onion. Cook over medium-high heat until onions are translucent, about 5 minutes.

2. Put the cabbage, zucchini, carrots, and apple in the slow cooker. Add the cooked onions. Add the chicken broth and wine, cover, and cook on Low for about 8 hours, or on High for 3 or 4 hours. Check the soup. The cabbage should be cooked but still fairly firm. Turn to Low, if on High, and cook for another 20 to 30 minutes until heated through.

3. Season with the salt and pepper. Stir and serve.

chicken soup with fennel and escarole

An easy-to-make chicken soup with the delicious hint of licorice from the fresh fennel. Escarole is a hearty green that contributes texture and flavor.

makes 6 to 8 servings ~~~~~~

1 pound (454 g) boneless, skinless chicken from thighs or breasts

1 large fennel bulb, cored and cut into squares

3 tablespoons olive oil

1 large white onion, diced

2 cloves garlic, minced

2 teaspoons fennel seeds, crushed

5 cups (1.3 L) low-fat chicken broth

1 head escarole, cored and shredded

Salt and pepper, to taste

1. Rinse chicken and pat dry with paper towels. Trim chicken of all visible fat, and cut into ½-inch (13 mm) cubes. Place chicken and fennel in the slow cooker.

2. Heat olive oil in a medium skillet over medium-high heat. Add onion and garlic and cook, stirring frequently, for about 5 minutes or until onion is translucent.

3. Put the onion mixture into the slow cooker, then the fennel seeds, then the broth. Stir to combine. Cook on Low for 5 to 7 hours or on High for 3 to 4 hours, or until chicken is cooked through and no longer pink.

4. If cooking on Low, raise heat to High. Add the escarole to the slow cooker and cook for an additional hour until escarole is wilted. Season with the salt and pepper and serve hot.

pumpkin and pear soup

Like sweet potatoes, pumpkin is a vibrant, fleshy, fibrous vegetable with a hint of sweetness that makes a delicious base for soup and stew. A pinch of turmeric brings out the pumpkin's beautiful color.

makes 6 servings

2 tablespoons butter

1 large onion, chopped

1 clove garlic crushed

1 teaspoon turmeric

2 pounds (1 kg) pumpkin (or butternut squash) peeled, seeded, and cut into 2-inch (5 cm) pieces

2 Bosc or Anjou pears, peeled, cored and cubed

2 carrots, peeled and cut into thin slices

6 cups (1.5 L) chicken broth

3 sprigs fresh thyme

Salt and pepper, to taste

6 fresh sage leaves

1. Heat the butter in a skillet and add the onions, and garlic, cooking over medium-high heat until translucent, about 3 to 5 minutes. Stir in the turmeric and remove from heat.

2. Into the slow cooker, add the pumpkin, pears, and carrots. Stir in the chicken broth. Add the cooked onions and stir. Put thyme on top. Cover and cook on Low for 6 to 8 hours or on High for 4 to 6 hours, or until vegetables and fruit are cooked through and soft. Remove the thyme sprigs.

3. Puree with an immersion blender or in batches in a food processor or blender. Season with the salt and pepper. Serve hot. Garnish with the sage leaves.

bean, corn, and barley soup

Barley is an ancient grain that is used in Italy's Northern provinces. It creates a thick and robust soup flavored with many vegetables and herbs, as well as cannellini beans.

makes 6 to 8 servings

1 tablespoon olive oil

1 medium onion, minced

2 cloves garlic, minced

1 celery rib, washed and sliced thin

¾ cup (150 g) pearl barley, rinsed well

5 cups (1.3 L) vegetable or chicken broth

¼ cup (32 g) fresh parsley, chopped

1 tablespoon fresh rosemary, chopped

1 bay leaf

1 15-ounce can (425 g) cannellini beans, drained and rinsed

¾ cup (130 g) fresh corn kernels or frozen kernels, thawed

Salt and pepper, to taste

1. Heat oil in a large skillet over medium-high heat. Add onion, garlic, and celery and cook, stirring, for about 5 minutes or until onion is translucent. Scrape mixture into the slow cooker.

2. Add the barley, broth, parsley, rosemary, and bay leaf to the slow cooker and stir well to combine. Cook on Low for 8 hours or on High for 4 hours, until vegetables are tender.

3. If cooking on Low, raise heat to High. Add the beans and corn, stir to combine, and cook for an additional 30 minutes.

4. Remove and discard bay leaf, and season with the salt and pepper. Serve hot.

watercress soup

If you like the tangy yet delicate flavor of watercress, you will love this soup, which is thickened with tofu. Substitute arugula if watercress is hard to find.

makes 8 to 10 servings

2 bunches watercress, washed, dried, and some stalk removed

1 cup (70 g) washed and shredded cabbage leaves

2 large portobello mushrooms, washed, patted dry, and chopped

6 cups (1.5 L) vegetable or chicken broth

2 cups (475 ml) water

¼ cup (32 g) cornstarch, dissolved in ¼ cup (60 ml) water (you can also use rice flour or arrowroot as a substitute for the cornstarch)

2 scallions, white part only, sliced thin

1 cup (125 g) tofu, cubed

1. Into the slow cooker, add the watercress, cabbage, mushrooms, broth, and water. Cover and cook on Low for 6 hours or on High for 3 hours. When liquid is bubbly and cooked through, stir in the dissolved cornstarch and continue stirring with slow cooker on High for a few minutes or until thoroughly blended.

2. Stir in the scallions and tofu, cover, and cook on Low for an additional 30 minutes. Serve hot.

For a slightly different version, add 1 can of chickpeas to the soup. If you prefer a creamier style, run it through a blender or food processor. Then place it back in the slow cooker for another 15 minutes on High to warm it back up. Garnish with chickpeas and dark bread croutons. Serve hot.

salmon chowder

Chowder is a traditional fisherman's stew—a thick, creamy stew full of potatoes and fish in a cream base (except for Manhattan clam chowder, which has a tomato base). This variation trades the hearty clam for smoked salmon, which is more delicate but has a nice umph.

makes 4 to 6 servings

¼ cup or ½ stick (60 g) unsalted butter

1 medium onion, minced

1 pound (454 g) Yukon Gold potatoes, peeled and cubed

3 cups (750 ml) milk, whole or 2% but not low-fat

2 cups (500 ml) water

1 teaspoon salt

½ teaspoon pepper

1 pound (454 g) salmon steak, skinned and boned

2 tablespoons flour

4 ounces (113 g) smoked salmon, chopped fine (optional)

2 tablespoons fresh dill, chopped, or 2 teaspoons dried dill, crumbled

1. In a large skillet, heat the butter over medium heat and cook the onion until translucent, about 5 minutes. Put the onion with the potatoes in the slow cooker, and add the milk and water. Sprinkle with the salt and pepper. Cover and cook on High for about 2 hours until the potatoes are tender.

2. When potatoes have about 30 minutes left to cook, put the salmon steak over the potato mixture and continue to cook on High. After 15 minutes, turn the salmon steak over and continue to cook another 15 to 20 minutes, until the fish is just cooked through.

3. Take a ladle of hot liquid from the slow cooker and put it in a skillet. Simmer over medium heat and stir in the flour until there are no lumps. Transfer the hot liquid back to the slow cooker. Reduce the heat to Low and cook another 20 to 30 minutes with the lid propped open with a wooden spoon so the chowder thickens.

4. Before serving, break the salmon steak into pieces. Ladle into bowls and top with the smoked salmon and dill.

manhattan clam chowder

This tomato-based version of chowder has as many devoted fans as the creamy version has in New England. The combination of the vegetables and herbs makes this recipe a real winner.

makes 6 to 8 servings

1 ½ pounds (680 grams) fresh minced clams whole small clams in shells

1 ½ pounds (680 g) small unshelled shrimp

2 tablespoons olive oil

1 large onion, minced

3 cloves garlic, minced

2 celery ribs, diced

1 carrot, finely chopped

½ green bell pepper, seeds and ribs removed, chopped

1 large turnip, peeled and cubed

1 28-ounce (794 g) can crushed tomatoes, undrained

2 8-ounce (240 ml) bottles clam juice

3 tablespoons chopped fresh parsley

1 tablespoon fresh thyme or ½ teaspoon dried

½ teaspoon dried oregano

2 bay leaves

Salt and pepper, to taste

Cayenne pepper (optional)

1. Drain clams, reserving juice. Refrigerate clams until ready to use.

2. Heat oil in a medium skillet over medium heat. Add onion, garlic, celery, carrot, and green bell pepper. Cook, stirring frequently, for about 5 minutes, or until onion is translucent. Scrape mixture into the slow cooker.

3. Add turnips, tomatoes (and juice), clam juice, reserved juice drained from clams, parsley, thyme, oregano, and bay leaves to the slow cooker, and stir well. Cook on Low for 5 to 7 hours or on High for 3 to 4 hours, or until turnips are almost tender.

4. Add clams, and continue cooking on High for an additional 20 to 40 minutes, or until clams are cooked through. Remove and discard bay leaves, season with the salt and pepper—and a dash of cayenne pepper, if desired—and serve hot.

chicken and corn soup

For a soup that's more of a flavorful broth, leave out the pasta or rice. If you want something thicker and with additional texture, include the pasta or rice.

2 tablespoons olive oil

2 large ribs celery, finely diced

1 medium onion, finely diced

1 pinch saffron threads

½ teaspoon dried thyme

¼ teaspoon cumin

Nonstick cooking spray

2 carrots, peeled and cut into thin slices

1 cup (125 g) frozen corn

8 cups (2 L) chicken broth

2 cups (250 g) finely diced or shredded cooked chicken

¼ cup (15 g) chopped fresh flat-leaf parsley

Salt and pepper, to taste

1. Heat the oil in a saucepan over medium heat. Add the celery, onion, saffron, thyme, and cumin. Cook, stirring occasionally, until the vegetables start to soften, about 5 minutes.

2. Spray the slow cooker. Put the vegetable mixture in it, and the carrots and corn, and add the broth.

3. Cover and cook on Low for about 5 hours and then on High for 3 hours. Add the chicken and replace the cover, cooking another 30 to 40 minutes on High. Add the parsley. Season with the salt and pepper and serve hot.

For a creamier version of this soup, add 1 cup (250 ml) heavy cream.

curried carrot soup

Curry and carrots are a perfect pairing, with the slight smoky-hot flavor of the curry complementing a sweet taste of carrots. If you can find high-quality Madras curry, it has a deeper flavor and a bit less heat than standard ground curry powder. No matter, you'll still have the great curry flavor.

makes 6 to 8 servings

2 tablespoons olive oil

2 medium onions, chopped

4 teaspoon curry powder

1 tablespoon fresh ginger, grated

3 pounds (1.4 kg) carrots, peeled and chopped

4 cups (1 L) vegetable or chicken broth

5 cups (1.3 L) water

Salt and pepper, to taste

Sour cream or crème fraiche, to garnish (optional)

1. Heat the oil in a skillet and add the onions, cooking over medium-high heat until the onion is translucent, about 3 to 5 minutes. Turn the heat to Low and add the curry powder and ginger, stirring constantly for about a minute to coat the onions. Remove the skillet from the heat.

2. Put the carrots in the slow cooker, and scrape the onion mixture on top. Cover with the broth and water.

3. Cook on Low for 4 to 5 hours or on High for 2 to 3 hours. Use an immersion blender to puree the soup, or process by batches in a blender. Season with the salt and pepper.

4. Serve hot with a dollop of sour cream or crème fraiche in the middle of the bowl, or on the side.

hot-and-sour soup

Why is it that we only enjoy this delicious soup when we're at a Chinese restaurant? It's easy enough to make at home—and so much fresher and more fragrant. The "hot" is chili oil, and the "sour" is vinegar and lemon juice. The result is tasty!

makes 4 to 6 servings

3 pounds (1.4 kg) boneless pork chops

½ onion, finely chopped

4 cloves garlic, minced

1 14.5-ounce (412 g) can bamboo shoots, drained

1 8-ounce (250 ml) can sliced water chestnuts, drained

2 tablespoons rice vinegar

1 teaspoon sesame seed oil

1 to 3 teaspoons hot chili oil, depending on how hot you like it

2 tablespoons lemon juice

2 tablespoons soy sauce

2 portobello mushrooms, sliced

2 cups (500 ml) chicken stock or broth

1 cup (250 ml) water

1. Place the pork chops on the bottom of the slow cooker, and cover with the onion and garlic.

2. Next, layer the bamboo shoots and water chestnuts on top of the chops. In a 2-cup (250 g) measuring cup or small bowl, combine the vinegar, sesame seed oil, chili oil, lemon juice, and soy sauce. Pour over the other ingredients in the slow cooker.

3. Add a layer of the portobello mushrooms, and cover everything with the chicken stock and water. Cook on Low for 5 to 7 hours or on High for 3 to 4 hours.

fennel and potato soup

A root vegetable—based soup with hints of licorice that is served cold on a hot summer day—with a glass of bubbly, of course! A mainstream variation on this recipe calls for lots of garlic, as well, to further enhance the flavor. If desired, try adding a small amount and, if your system can handle it, increase the number of cloves, but don't add more than six per batch.

makes 6 to 8 servings

2 tablespoons olive oil

½ large or 1 medium onion, diced

2 stalks celery, sliced

2 pounds (900 g) bulb fennel, trimmed, washed and diced (fronds reserved for garnish)

Nonstick cooking spray

Salt and pepper, to taste

1 pound (454 g) Yukon gold potatoes, peeled and diced

2 to 6 garlic cloves, peeled and halved

A bouquet garni made with a bay leaf, a couple of sprigs each parsley and thyme, and ½ teaspoon fennel seeds, tied in cheesecloth

2 cups (475 ml) water, vegetable stock, or chicken broth

Chopped fresh fennel fronds, for garnish

Crème fraiche, for garnish

½ cup (50 g) chopped green onions (optional)

1. Heat the olive oil in a large saucepan over medium heat and add the onion, celery, chopped fennel, and season with the salt and pepper. Cook gently for about 5 to 8 minutes, until the vegetables have softened.

2. Spray the slow cooker with the cooking spray. Add the potatoes, garlic, bouquet garni, cooked vegetable mixture, and the water or stock. Cover and cook 5 to 7 hours on Low or 2 to 3 hours on High.

3. Remove the bouquet garni. Blend the soup until smooth with an immersion blender, or puree in batches in a food processor or blender. Transfer to a container and allow to chill. Cover and refrigerate several hours to serve cold. Garnish with the fennel fronds and crème fraiche or with chopped green onions.

creamy broccoli soup

This recipe makes a bright green soup that lets the flavor of the broccoli shine through. Add a drizzle of sesame oil for some extra goodness on the finish.

makes 6 to 8 servings

¼ cup or ½ stick (60 g) butter

1 onion, minced

2 large heads, approximately 8 cups (560 g), broccoli, trimmed of coarse stalk and cut into chunks

6 cups (1.5 L) chicken stock or broth

1 cup (250 ml) heavy cream

1 teaspoon salt

½ teaspoon pepper

Sesame oil, to drizzle (optional)

1. In a skillet over medium-high heat, melt the butter and cook the onion until translucent, about 5 minutes. Transfer onion to the slow cooker.

2. Add the broccoli, then the chicken stock. Stir to combine. Cover and cook on Low for about 6 hours or on High for about 4 hours, until broccoli is tender and cooked through.

3. Puree the broccoli with an immersion blender or by processing in batches in a blender.

4. Add the cream, salt, and pepper, stir, and keep the heat on until heated through. Season with additional salt and pepper, if desired. Serve hot with sesame oil on the side for a delicious drizzle.

asian squash soup

Lemongrass is native to India, but is grown worldwide and is a common ingredient in the cuisines of Thailand and Vietnam. Not only is it aromatic, it has numerous health benefits, including as a digestive aid, for flatulence, to boost the immune system, and as a detoxing agent for the liver, kidneys, and digestive organs.

makes 4 to 6 servings

1 tablespoon olive oil

2 onions, diced

2 stalks lemongrass

4 cloves garlic, minced

2 tablespoons minced fresh ginger

1 teaspoon peppercorns

1 tablespoon cumin

1 large butternut squash, peeled, seeds removed, and cut into cubes

6 cups (1.5 L) chicken stock or broth

1 13.5-ounce (400 ml) can coconut milk, with

2 tablespoons reserved

4 ounces (113 g) red curry paste

Zest and juice of 1 lime

1 cup (60 g) chopped fresh cilantro

1. In a skillet over medium-high heat, heat the olive oil and cook the onions until translucent, about 5 minutes.

2. Trim the lemongrass stalks and cut them in half lengthwise down the middle. Add these, the garlic, ginger, peppercorns, and cumin to the onions, and stir to heat through, about 1 minute.

3. Put the butternut squash in the slow cooker, and top with the onion and spice mix.

4. In a large bowl, combine the chicken stock and coconut milk, pour over the other ingredients in the slow cooker, cover, and cook on Low for 5 to 6 hours or on High for 2 to 3 hours.

5. Keeping the slow cooker on warm, remove lemongrass stalks and discard. In a small bowl, combine the reserved 2 tablespoons coconut milk with the red curry paste and add this to the soup, along with the lime juice and zest, stirring to combine.

6. Puree the soup using an immersion blender or working in batches to puree in a blender, returning the pureed mix to the slow cooker to keep it warm. When ready to serve, ladle into bowls and garnish with fresh cilantro.

bouillabaise

*This is an amazing one-pot meal of assorted fish and shellfish that makes for a fun and festive meal on a summer night. This classic French fish "boil" is said to have originated in the seaside town of Marseilles in the south of France. The word itself has a fanciful attribution—*bouille-abbesse, *or the abbess' boil—in reference to a particular abbesse in a convent there; and the more practical* bouillon abaissé, *meaning, "to reduce by evaporation." Be sure to have a big loaf of crusty French bread to eat with it!*

makes 6 to 8 servings

1 onion, chopped

3 cloves garlic, minced

2 stalks celery, fronds removed, finely chopped

1 red pepper, seeded and chopped

1 cup (250 ml) fish stock (or clam juice)

½ cup (120 ml) water

2 tablespoons extra virgin olive oil

1 tablespoon lemon zest

1 tablespoon fresh basil, chopped

1 tablespoon fresh parsley, chopped

1 teaspoon fresh oregano

1 teaspoon fresh thyme, chopped

1 bay leaf

1 pound (454 g) firm white fish, cut into 1-inch (2.5 cm) pieces

¾ pound (340 g) shelled, cleaned shrimp, tails removed

½ pound squid (225 g), cleaned and sliced

1 6½-ounce (154 ml) can chopped clams with juice

½ pound (225 g) cleaned, fresh crab meat

Salt and pepper, to taste

¼ cup (15 g) fresh parsley, chopped

1. In a large bowl, combine onion, garlic, celery, red pepper, fish stock, water, olive oil, zest, spices, and bay leaf. Combine well. Put into slow cooker.

2. Cover and cook on Low for 6 hours or on High for 4 hours until base is hot and flavors are combined. Reduce heat to Low. Stir in fish, shrimp, clams, squid, and crab and cook for an additional 45 minutes to 1 hour, or until fish is done. Remove bay leaf and season with the salt and pepper, before serving. Stir in or garnish with parsley.

can't-miss beef stew

Slow-cooked beef stew is such a treat. There's something that happens to the vegetables when they cook in the fat and juices from the beef for hours, making magic from these simple ingredients.

2 tablespoons olive oil

1 onion, finely chopped

2 cloves garlic, minced

3 to 4 pounds (1.3 kg to 1.8 kg) chuck or bottom round beef

½ teaspoon salt

½ teaspoon pepper

4 carrots, sliced

½ pound (225 g) green beans, tops and bottoms snipped, and cut into 2-inch (5 cm) pieces

2 large potatoes, peeled and cubed

4 cups (1 L) beef stock or broth

1 bay leaf

1 teaspoon flour or cornstarch for thickener, if desired

1. Heat the oil in a skillet and add the onions and garlic, cooking over medium-high heat until the onion is translucent, about 3 to 5 minutes. Use a slotted spoon to scoop out the mix, and put it into the slow cooker.

2. Turn the heat up under the skillet and, with the grease left from cooking the onions, brown the pieces of beef on all sides, working in batches if necessary. Allow 2 or so minutes per side or cube, just to evenly brown them.

3. Transfer the beef to the slow cooker and sprinkle with salt and pepper. Add carrots, beans, potato, bay leaf, and pour beef stock over everything.

4. Cover and cook on Low for 6 to 8 hours or on High for 4 to 5 hours. If you like a thicker sauce, when the stew is cooked, take out about a half cup of the juices and mix in the flour or cornstarch. Pour back into the stew and stir to combine. Remove the bay leaf. Let sit for 10 to 15 minutes on warm before serving.

lamb and carrot stew

For those who love the flavor of lamb, this is a great alternative to beef stew. Lamb has an earthy flavor that imbues a stew such as this with an extra umph. The Middle Eastern spices—cumin, coriander, and even cinnamon—help create an exotic treat.

makes 6 to 8 servings

2 pounds (1 kg) boneless leg of lamb

1 onion, minced

3 cloves garlic, minced

4 medium carrots, sliced

1 large potato, peeled and cubed

1 bulb fennel, cored and sliced into thin strips

1 tablespoon cumin

1 tablespoon coriander

1 teaspoon cayenne pepper

1 teaspoon cinnamon

1 cup (250 ml) chicken broth or water

1. Trim excess fat off of the lamb, leaving some to flavor the meat and contribute to the sauce. Cut the meat into large chunks. Put it in the slow cooker.

2. Sprinkle the onion and garlic over the meat, then add the carrots, potato, and fennel. In a small bowl, combine the spices and stir to combine thoroughly. Sprinkle the spice mixture over the meat. Top with the broth or water.

3. Cover and cook on Low for 7 to 8 hours or on High for 4 to 5 hours.

lots-of-beef chili

It's fall, it's football season, the game of the week is on tonight, and this is the chili you want to serve. Make it in the morning, and you have nothing to do but serve with assorted toppings, get the beer cold, and watch the game later.

makes 4 to 6 servings

1 tablespoon olive oil

1 pound (454 g) lean ground beef

1 pound (454 g) chuck or round steak, cut into bite-size pieces

1 large onion, diced

5 cloves garlic, minced

1 tablespoon salt

1 tablespoon chili powder

1 teaspoon cumin

1 teaspoon cayenne

1 15-ounce (425 g) can red kidney beans

1 28-ounce (794 ml) can crushed tomatoes

1 8-ounce (227 g) can tomato sauce

3 cups (750 ml) beef broth

Shredded Cheddar cheese, to top

Sour cream, to top

1. In a large skillet, heat the oil and brown the ground beef until cooked through. Use a slotted spoon to scoop the cooked meat into the slow cooker.

2. Add the beef cubes to the skillet and cook, turning, until they are browned on all sides, about 6 minutes. Transfer them to the slow cooker with the slotted spoon. Cook the onions and garlic in the skillet until the onions are translucent, about 3 minutes. Add them to the slow cooker.

3. Put the spices, beans, tomatoes, tomato sauce, and broth into the slow cooker. Cover and cook on Low for 8 hours or on High for 5 hours.

4. Serve with shredded Cheddar, sour cream, and other toppings of your choice.

turkey-corn chili

The lean turkey meat needs some extra ingredients to keep the flavor kicked up—including peppers, corn, and lots of spices. Topped with ripe avocados and cheese and served with warm tortillas, this one is a winner.

makes 6 to 8 servings

1 pound (454 g) lean ground turkey

1 large onion, chopped

3 cloves garlic, minced

2 cups (250 g) frozen corn kernels

1 green bell pepper, seeded and cut into small squares

1 jalapeno pepper, seeds removed, sliced thin

1 28-ounce (794 ml) can diced tomatoes

1 15-ounce (425 g) can red beans, rinsed and drained

1 8-ounce (227 g) can tomato sauce

2 tablespoons chili powder

1 teaspoon cumin

1 teaspoon cayenne

½ teaspoon salt

¼ teaspoon pepper

Shredded Cheddar cheese

1. In a large skillet, brown the turkey until almost cooked through. Stir in the onions and garlic, continuing to cook until there is no more pink color. Remove from heat but do not drain.

2. Put the meat, onion and garlic mix into the slow cooker. Stir in the corn, green bell pepper, jalapeno pepper, tomatoes, beans, tomato sauce, and spices.

3. Cover and cook on Low for 8 hours or on High for 5 hours. Serve with shredded cheese.

For a slightly different version, more flavorful version, add 1 whole avocado, peeled, pitted, and sliced thin.

side dishes:
pasta, potatoes, and rice

easy risotto

Risotto is traditionally made by stirring liquid into the rice slowly as it cooks on the stovetop. In this recipe, the rice is started that way but is finished in the slow cooker. Brilliant!

makes 4 servings

3 tablespoons unsalted butter

1 medium white onion, chopped

1 cup (195 g) Arborio rice

3 cups (709 ml) chicken broth

½ cup (40 g) Parmesan cheese

Salt and pepper, to taste

1. Heat butter in a medium saucepan over medium-high heat. Add onion and cook, stirring frequently, for 3 minutes or until onion is translucent.

2. Add rice and stir to coat grains. Raise the heat to High and add about ¼ cup to ½ cup (250 ml to 500 ml) broth. Stir for about two minutes, or until it is almost evaporated. Scrape mixture into the slow cooker.

3. Add the remaining broth to the slow cooker and stir well. Cook on High for 2 hours or until rice is soft and liquid is absorbed. Stir in cheese and season with the salt and pepper. Serve hot.

Arborio rice is uniquely Italian, and is named after the town in which it was developed. It is a short, fat grain with a pearly white exterior and high starch content, the result of less milling. Another characteristic is its ability to absorb flavors.

mad-good mushroom risotto

There's something magical about the combination of earthy mushrooms and creamy risotto. It's a comfort food dish like no other, made all the more delightful by being cooked in the slow cooker.

makes 4 servings

6 tablespoons unsalted butter or 4 tablespoons butter and 2 tablespoons olive oil, divided

1 medium onion, chopped

1 cup (195 g) Arborio rice

3 cups (750 ml) chicken broth, divided

1 cup (70 g) domestic mushrooms, trimmed and sliced

1 cup (70 g) portobello mushrooms, cut into 1-inch (2.5 cm) cubes

½ cup (40 g) Parmesan cheese

Salt and pepper, to taste

Sprig of thyme, for garnish

1. Heat 4 tablespoons of butter in a medium saucepan over medium-high heat. Add onion and cook, stirring frequently, for 3 minutes, or until onion is translucent.

2. Add rice and stir to coat grains. Raise the heat to High and add about ¼ cup to ½ cup (250 ml to 500 ml) broth. Stir for about 2 minutes, or until it is almost evaporated. Scrape mixture into the slow cooker.

3. In the skillet, add another 2 tablespoons of butter or olive oil and sauté the mushrooms for about 2 minutes or until they are just soft, stirring constantly. Add the mushrooms to the slow cooker, then the remaining broth, and stir well. Cook on High for 2 to 3 hours or until rice is soft and liquid is absorbed.

4. Stir in cheese, season with salt and pepper, and serve hot. Garnish with sprig of thyme.

risotto with asparagus

This is a delicious springtime dish. The green asparagus tips are bright and fresh and delicious. When preparing the asparagus, use only the tips for this recipe as they are the tastiest and most tender. Reserve the green stems for steaming or adding to soup.

makes 4 servings

3 tablespoons unsalted butter

1 medium white
onion, chopped

1 cup (195 g) Arborio rice

3 cups (750 ml) chicken broth

1 cup (135 g) asparagus tips
(about ½ inch, or 13 mm, long)

½ cup (40 g)
Parmesan cheese

Salt and pepper, to taste

1. Heat butter in a medium saucepan over medium-high heat. Add onion and cook, stirring frequently, for 3 minutes, or until onion is translucent.

2. Add rice and stir to coat grains. Raise the heat to High and add about ¼ cup to ½ cup (59 ml to 188 ml) broth. Stir for about 2 minutes, or until it is almost evaporated. Scrape mixture into the slow cooker.

3. Add the remaining broth to the slow cooker and stir well. Cook on High for 2 hours or until rice is soft and liquid is absorbed.

4. Stir in the asparagus tips and cook for another 20 to 30 minutes. Add the cheese and season with the salt and pepper. Serve hot.

herbed polenta

Polenta hails from Italy, though it wasn't developed until corn started coming in from the New World. It's a corn "oatmeal" of sorts, and in this country it's most often cooked up for breakfast in place of grits, though it's developing more and more of a following in culinary circles.

makes 4 servings

Nonstick cooking spray

5 cups (1.3 L)
chicken broth

1 cup (250 ml) milk

1 cup (140 g) polenta
(yellow corn meal)

½ teaspoon fresh
parsley, chopped

½ teaspoon fresh
thyme, chopped

½ teaspoon fresh
rosemary, chopped

3 tablespoons unsalted butter

1 cup (120 g) grated
Cheddar cheese

Salt and pepper, to taste

1. Spray the slow cooker liberally with the nonstick cooking spray. Combine the broth, milk, and polenta in the slow cooker. Whisk together thoroughly, cover, and cook on High for about 1½ hours, or until mixture begins to boil.

2. Open the lid and add the herbs. Whisk again, cover and cook on High an additional 1½ hours, then turn heat to Low and cook for 2 to 3 more hours, or until polenta is very thick.

3. Stir in the butter and cheese, and season with the salt and pepper. Serve hot.

An alternative way to serve polenta is to pack the hot polenta into a well-oiled loaf pan and chill it well. Once chilled you can cut it into slices and either grill or sauté them in butter or olive oil. You can also spread the polenta in a shallow baking dish to the thickness of ¾ inch, (2 cm) and then chill the mixture, cut it into long, narrow rectangles, and pan-fry them.

mashed potatoes

There's something utterly satisfying about mashed potatoes. The flavor, the texture—everything. It's easy to make them in a slow cooker, mashing in the delicious butter, cream, salt and pepper just before you're ready to serve them.

makes 8 to 10 servings ~~~~~~~~~~~~~~~~~~~~~~~~~~~~~~~

10 large golden potatoes, peeled and cubed

7 cups (1.8 L) chicken stock or broth

1 cup (250 ml) light cream, warmed

1 cup or 2 sticks (240 g) salted butter, cut into pieces

1 teaspoon salt (plus more, to taste)

½ teaspoon pepper (and more, to taste)

1. Put the potatoes and chicken stock in the slow cooker. Cover and cook on Low for about 6 hours or on High for about 4 hours, or until potatoes are tender.

2. With the slow cooker on warm, mash the potatoes with ¾ cup of the cream and the butter. Add salt and pepper and stir. Add additional cream, if needed, for desired consistency. Season with additional salt and pepper, if necessary.

Leftover mashed potatoes are wonderful to add to soups to thicken them. You can also form leftover mashed potatoes into small "cakes" and fry them in butter. Garnishing them with fresh chopped parsley is always a tasty treat.

baked potatoes

These are another crowd favorite, and not only do they cook up nicely in the slow cooker, but they can be kept warm there, too, giving you some leeway in the timing of your meal.

makes 4 to 8 servings

4 to 8 russet potatoes
(quantity will vary depending
on the size of the potatoes
and your slow cooker)

Aluminum foil

1. Wash and dry the potatoes. Wrap each potato in foil. Place the potatoes in the slow cooker.

2. Cook on Low for about 8 hours until tender when pierced with a knife.

Classic accompaniments to baked potatoes include butter (of course!), salt and pepper (definitely!), sour cream, and chives. You could do a baked potato toppings bar, though, and make the potatoes a really fun part of a buffet. Additional toppings include crumbled bacon, Cheddar cheese, blue cheese, sautéed onions, sautéed mushrooms, steamed broccoli bits, or caviar if you want to get really fancy.

roasted (but not) red potatoes

With long slow cooking, you'll be pleased to discover that small red potatoes will even get a bit crispy around the edges. If they don't and you want them slightly crispy, put them on a cookie sheet and bake in a 400°F (200°C) oven for about 10 minutes, shaking them about halfway through so they crisp evenly. The garlic and rosemary are delicious additions, and pair exceptionally well with pork, lamb, or beef.

makes 4 to 6 servings

6 tablespoons olive oil

8 small red potatoes, skins on and scrubbed clean

4 cloves garlic, minced

1 tablespoon fresh rosemary, coarsely chopped

1 teaspoon salt

½ teaspoon pepper

1. Put the oil in the slow cooker, cover, and set to High. Cut the potatoes in half, while the oil heats, about 15 minutes.

2. Add the potatoes, garlic, rosemary, salt, and pepper to the slow cooker and stir well, getting everything mixed and the potatoes well covered with the oil and seasonings.

3. Reduce heat to Low and cook for 5 to 6 hours, or keep heat on High and cook for about 3 hours, or until potatoes are tender. The skins should be browned. Season with the salt and pepper.

Use flavored oils to vary this recipe. Try using olive oils infused with roasted garlic, truffle, basil, or hot peppers (or a combination). You'll want to omit the rosemary with anything but the roasted garlic or hot pepper oils, and you could add ½ cup (35 g) diced portobello mushrooms if you choose the truffle oil.

cheesy scalloped potatoes

Once you have the potatoes peeled and sliced, it's just a matter of stacking them in the slow cooker, adding the other ingredients, and returning a masterpiece.

makes 4 servings

Nonstick cooking spray

6 medium Idaho potatoes, peeled and thinly sliced

1 onion, thinly sliced

1 cup (120 g) shredded Cheddar cheese

½ cup (30 g) fresh parsley, minced

½ cup (112 ml) milk

½ cup or 1 stick (120 g) salted butter, melted

½ teaspoon paprika

Salt and pepper, to taste

1. Spray the slow cooker liberally with the nonstick cooking spray.

2. In the slow cooker, alternate layers of potatoes, onions, cheese, and parsley until all are used up. In a small bowl, combine the milk, butter, paprika, and season with the salt and pepper. Pour this mixture over the ingredients in the slow cooker.

3. Cover and cook on Low for 7 to 9 hours or on High for 3 to 4 hours until potatoes are cooked through and bubbly. Serve hot.

This dish is classically prepared with heavy cream and lots of butter. While this makes an especially creamy dish, scalloped potatoes can be just as satisfying with far less fat and calories, as this recipe proves. The slow cooking renders the thinly sliced potatoes tender and tasty.

slow-cooked rice

The secret to successful rice is letting it cook without lifting the lid—with the slow cooker, that's even less of a temptation, which is an advantage. You'll want to be sure to rub butter around the edges of the slow cooker so there is moisture and flavor on the outside, where the rice will cook faster than on the inside.

makes 4 servings ～～～～～～～～～～～～～～～～～～～～～～～～

2 tablespoons salted butter

1 cup (195 g) white rice

2 cups (500 ml) water

Salt and pepper, to taste

1. Rub the butter along the bottom and sides of the slow cooker. Add the rice and water. Stir gently.

2. Cook on Low for 4 hours or on High for 2 hours.

3. If the rice isn't fully cooked when you open the slow cooker, give it a gentle stir and continue to cook for about 30 minutes.

4. Season with the salt and pepper.

herbed wild rice

This is a nice side dish for roast chicken. While the chicken is roasting in the oven, the rice is cooking in the slow cooker, and your stovetop is free. No need to return frequently to the kitchen to check on anything. When the chicken and rice are ready, toss a nice green salad together, and you have dinner.

makes 4 servings

2 tablespoons salted butter

½ cup (80 g) chopped white onion

1 cup (125 g) wild rice

½ teaspoon dried basil, crushed

¼ teaspoon dried thyme, crushed

¼ teaspoon dried rosemary, crushed

1 clove garlic, minced

2½ cups (625 ml) vegetable or chicken broth

Salt and pepper, to taste

1. In a skillet over medium heat, sauté the onion in 1 tablespoon of the butter until soft, about 3 minutes.

2. Use the additional tablespoon of butter to rub the bottom and sides of the slow cooker.

3. Transfer the sautéed onion to the slow cooker. Add the rice, herbs, and garlic. Pour the broth over the mixture and gently stir to combine.

4. Cover and cook on Low for 6 to 7 hours or on High for 3 to 3½ hours. Stir and season with the salt and pepper, before serving.

baked ziti

Are there enough days in the week for a fabulous dish of baked ziti? Not on my calendar. This recipe is great because you don't have to cook the pasta ahead of time.

makes 4 to 6 servings

1 28-ounce (490 g) can crushed tomatoes (no seasoning)

1 15-ounce (300 g) can tomato sauce

½ teaspoon dried oregano

1 teaspoon dried basil

1 teaspoon salt

½ teaspoon pepper

1 teaspoon onion powder

2 cloves garlic, pressed

1 teaspoon red pepper flakes (optional)

1 pound (454 g) penne or ziti, uncooked

2 cups (230 g) shredded mozzarella cheese or 1 cup (115 g) shredded mozzarella and 1 cup (115 g) pizza blend cheese

1. In a bowl, combine the crushed tomatoes, tomato sauce, oregano, basil, salt, pepper, onion powder, crushed garlic, and red pepper flakes. Stir to combine thoroughly.

2. Pour about one-third of the sauce into the slow cooker. Add half of the pasta on top. Add another third tomato sauce. Next, sprinkle with about ½ cup (60 g) cheese. Add the remaining pasta, then sauce, then the rest of the cheese.

3. Cover and cook on Low for 4 hours or on High for 2 hours until pasta is cooked through and sauce is bubbling.

If you are asked to bring baked ziti to a party, it's great to make it in the slow cooker because you can just transport the whole thing there, keeping it on warm at the party instead of worrying about reheating it. If it's going to be sitting out for a while, bring a pasta sauce to serve on the side in case it gets dry.

savory stuffing

Even if you stuff your bird, it's great to have an extra dish of stuffing. Using the slow cooker to prepare it frees up that much more room in your oven. And the stuffing is nice and moist.

makes 8 to 10 servings

1 pound (454 g) Italian sausage, sweet, spicy, or a combination

3 large Granny Smith or Empire apples, peeled and cored

1 large onion, diced

1 cup (125 g) diced celery

6 cups (750 g) bread crumbs or 10 cups (1.3 kg) dried bread cubes

1 teaspoon fresh thyme, chopped

1 teaspoon salt

½ teaspoon pepper

3 eggs

6 cups (1.5 L) chicken stock or broth

1 cup or 2 sticks (240 g) salted butter, cut into pieces

¼ cup (15 g) fresh parsley, chopped

Salt and pepper, to taste

1. Cut sausages into bite-size pieces or cut casings and remove meat so that it is loose. In a large skillet over medium-high heat, cook sausage until browned and cooked through.

2. Transfer cooked meat to a large bowl with a slotted spoon. Pour off all but ¼ cup (32 g) fat from skillet. Add the apples, onion, and celery, and cook, stirring, until onions are translucent, about 5 minutes. Add the onion mix to the bowl with the sausage.

3. Stir the bread crumbs or cubed bread into the bowl with the sausage and onion mix. Add thyme, salt, and pepper, stirring to combine. Put seasoned bread into the slow cooker.

4. In the bowl in which the bread mixture was prepared, whisk the eggs together lightly and add the chicken stock. Whisk briefly to combine. Pour over bread mixture. Dot with the butter pieces.

5. Cover and cook on Low for 6 to 8 hours or on High for 4 to 5 hours. Transfer to a bowl to serve, season with the salt and pepper, garnish with the chopped parsley.

There are lots of variations to stuffing recipes. Some of the popular additions include dried fruits such as raisins or cranberries; nuts like toasted pine nuts, chestnuts, or walnuts; oysters; or squash. A traditional preparation tends to please the most people, and also makes a great addition to soup.

side dishes: vegetables

artichokes with lemon and herbs

The slow cooker is the perfect way to make great artichokes, which need to be cooked so that the insides are soft but the leaves are still somewhat firm.

makes 6 servings

4 to 6 artichokes, depending on size of vegetables and the slow cooker

1 lemon, quartered

3 cloves garlic, peeled and crushed

1 teaspoon fresh rosemary, minced

2 cups (500 ml) water

1. Wash and pat dry the artichokes. Trim the stem to about ¼ inch (6 mm) from bottom. Pull off the first couple of layers of leaves at the bottom, and snip the pointy ends off the leaves all around the artichokes.

2. Place the artichokes in the slow cooker, bottoms down. Squeeze the juice of the lemons over the artichokes and put the squeezed quarters in with the artichokes, distributed throughout. Put the garlic cloves in the slow cooker, distributed throughout. Sprinkle the rosemary around the artichokes.

3. Pour the water around the artichokes so that it covers the bottom of the slow cooker with about ½-inch to 1-inch (1.25 cm to 2.5 cm) of water. Cover and cook on Low for 6 to 8 hours or on High for 4 to 5 hours. Artichokes should be tender, with leaves easily breaking away from the core. Serve hot or at room temperature with the lemon/garlic juice as a dipping sauce for the leaves.

Artichokes are a lot of fun to eat as you work your way through the leaves to what is considered the vegetable's most delicious part, its heart. Peel each leaf off and dip the bottom into the lemon/garlic cooking liquid, or into some melted coconut butter. Put the leaf in your mouth, press down with your teeth, and scrape the tender flesh from the lower part of the leaves. Work through the artichoke until the leaves are small and nearly transparent. Pull off the last tip of leaves. The heart will be left, attached to the stem. There is some "fuzz" on the top of the heart that needs to be gently scraped off, as it can be bitter. It falls off easily. Now enjoy the heart!

roasted tomatoes

Because the slow cooker retains the moisture in foods, these won't need to cook long to become moist and flavorful. Seasoned with some herbs and garlic, they make a colorful and tasty side dish.

makes 4 to 6 servings

4 large, ripe tomatoes, cut in half, seeds removed

2 cloves garlic, minced

1 teaspoon fresh oregano, minced, or ½ teaspoon, dried

Salt and pepper, to taste

1 teaspoon fresh parsley, chopped

Place cut tomatoes bottom down in the slow cooker. Sprinkle minced garlic on top, then sprinkle with the oregano. Cover and cook on Low for 3 to 4 hours or on High for 1 to 2 hours. Season with the salt and pepper, and garnish with the parsley.

Summer-ripe tomatoes taste too good to cook—use them in salads, salsas, or to stuff with some meat or vegetable mix. Slow cooking is great for off-season tomatoes, preferably vine-ripened.

glazed carrots

Adding a hint of something sweet to slow-cooked carrots turns them from tasty to terrific.

2 pounds (1 kg) carrots, peeled and cut quartered lengthwise into 4-inch (10 cm) sticks

½ cup (120 ml) vegetable broth or water

1 tablespoon sugar or maple syrup

1 teaspoon olive oil

2 tablespoons fresh parsley, dill, or thyme, chopped

1. Place carrot sticks in slow cooker. In a small bowl, combine the broth or water, sugar or syrup, and olive oil. Pour the liquid over the carrots.

2. Cover and cook on Low for 2 to 3 hours until carrots are tender. Open the lid and keep it propped open with the handle of a wooden spoon, and continue to cook for 20 to 30 minutes until some liquid is cooked off and the carrots glaze. Garnish with fresh herbs before serving.

Carrots could be considered "candy"—a vegetable that also has a fairly high sugar content. Fortunately that sugar is naturally occurring and a "treat" in the truest sense of the word. Carrots are loaded with other vitamins and minerals, most notably beta carotene, from which they get their color. The brighter the better!

italian-style peppers

This recipe is sooooooooo easy! You'll love it! Slice the bell peppers, toss them with some olive oil and garlic, put everything in the slow cooker, and return to a mountain of tender bell peppers that are the perfect accompaniment to any roast or other simple meat or fish dishes.

makes 8 to 10 servings

6 to 8 bell peppers (use a combo of green, red, yellow, and orange for the most color and flavor)

4 tablespoons olive oil

1 teaspoon salt

½ teaspoon pepper

2 tablespoons balsamic vinegar

1. Prepare the bell peppers by cutting out the core and removing all seeds. Slice the bell peppers into ¼-inch (6 mm) wide long strips.

2. In a large bowl, combine olive oil, salt, pepper, and balsamic vinegar. Add the bell peppers and stir to coat thoroughly. Put the bell peppers into the slow cooker. Cover and cook on Low for 5 to 7 hours or on High for 3 to 4 hours until tender and fragrant.

A great and fun way to serve Italian-style peppers is to toast Italian bread slices and layer some goat cheese and the peppers. Top with fresh basil!

brussels sprouts with bacon

Slow cooking this earthy veggie mellows its tanginess but brings out its woodsy depth of flavor. The smoky bacon, a touch of mustard, and seasoning with just a hint of sea salt add the perfect finish.

makes 4 to 6 servings

2 pounds (1 kg)
Brussels sprouts

½ pound (230 g)
thick-cut bacon

3 tablespoons olive oil

1 teaspoon dry mustard

½ cup (120 ml) water

Pinch sea salt

1. Wash and trim the Brussels sprouts, cutting off the coarsest part of the bottom and a layer or so of the leaves on the bottom. Cut the sprouts in half, and put them in the slow cooker.

2. In a large skillet, cook the slices of bacon over medium-high heat, turning to cook both sides until crisp. Drain on a plate covered with a paper towel and allow to cool.

3. In a measuring cup, combine the olive oil, dry mustard, and water. Pour over the Brussels sprouts. Sprinkle with crumbled bacon. Cover and cook on Low for 3 to 4 hours or on High for 2 to 3 hours. Before serving, add a pinch of sea salt.

While the mustard and bacon combine for a wonderful tanginess to this recipe, you can omit the bacon and substitute other spices to get different flavors. For spicier sprouts, add some cayenne pepper or Asian chili sauce; for an Indian taste, add hints of curry or cumin.

roasted beets

If you love beets, you'll love this method of cooking them. It "beats" waiting a long time for them to cook in boiling water!

4 to 5 medium-size beets with tops, (approximately 1 pound, or 454 g)

2 tablespoons olive oil

1 clove garlic, minced

Greens from the beets, washed and cut into 1-inch (2.5 cm) pieces

Salt, to taste

1. Scrub the beets clean. Cut the greens off, wash them and, cut them into 1-inch (2.5 cm) pieces. Peel the tough outer layer off the bulb.

2. Heat the oil in a medium skillet over medium-high heat and add the garlic. Cook, stirring constantly, about 1 minute. Add the beet greens and continue cooking and stirring until greens are just wilted, about 3 minutes.

3. Put beets into the slow cooker, topping with the greens. Cover and cook on Low for 4 to 5 hours, or on High for 3 to 4 hours, or until beets are soft.

4. Season with salt and serve.

Betacynin is the name of the pigment that gives red beets their deep color. Some people's bodies aren't able to process betacynin during digestion. As a result, their urine may be colored pink. This is temporary and is in no way harmful.

broccoli rabe

Consider this your "lazy" way to make great broccoli rabe. The longer this slow-cooks, the better, and if you put it on warm after 8 hours, it can go a few more hours. Or you can make it several days ahead and refrigerate until ready to reheat and serve.

makes 4 to 6 servings

1 pound (454 g) broccoli rabe

6 large cloves garlic, sliced

1 teaspoon red pepper flakes

⅓ cup (80 ml) extra virgin olive oil

Salt, to taste

1. Prepare the broccoli rabe by removing the tough stems and setting aside only the tops and the tender parts of the stems. Put these in a colander and rinse, then spin and pat dry.

2. Put the prepared broccoli rabe in the slow cooker, add the garlic, red pepper flakes, and olive oil. Cover and cook on Low for 6 to 8 hours. Do not cook on High. Season with salt to taste.

Broccoli rabe is related to broccoli, and is a member of the turnip family. It is definitely more bitter than broccoli, and has long been popular in Italy and Portugal.

A nice variation is to sprinkle pine nuts on top of the finished dish for added texture and flavor. A dash of red pepper flakes will give it more zing!

braised fennel and chard

Fennel has an almost silky texture and sweet flavor once it's braised. Swiss chard is a hearty green that adds a touch of color and lots of extra vitamins.

makes 4 to 6 servings

2 medium fennel bulbs

2 tablespoons butter

½ small onion, thinly sliced

1 clove garlic, minced

1 cup (240 ml) vegetable stock or broth

1 teaspoon fresh thyme, or ¼ teaspoon dried

1 pound (454 g) Swiss chard, coarse stems removed, and ripped into large pieces

Salt and pepper, to taste

1. Cut stalks off fennel bulb, trim root end, and cut bulb in half through the root. Trim out core, then slice fennel into 1-inch-thick (2.5 cm) slices across the bulb. Arrange slices in the slow cooker, and repeat with second bulb.

2. Heat butter in a small skillet over medium heat. Add onion and garlic and cook, stirring frequently, for 3 minutes, or until onion is translucent. Scrape mixture into the slow cooker.

3. Add stock and thyme to the slow cooker. Cook on Low for 3 to 4 hours or on High for about 2 hours, or until fennel is tender. Add the Swiss chard and continue to cook on Low for another 2 hours, or on High for another hour. Season with the salt and pepper.

Although the celery-like stalks are trimmed off the fennel bulb for this dish, don't throw them out. They add a wonderful anise flavor as well as a crisp texture when used in place of celery in salads and other raw dishes.

lean green beans

Fibrous and crunchy green beans turn into succulent and flavorful green beans when made in the slow cooker. Finding and cooking fresh beans is always best. This is a slow-roast method that tenderizes and retains flavor. The cherry tomatoes add lovely color and more flavor. And it's so easy!

makes 4 to 6 servings

2 pounds (1 kg) fresh green beans

8 to 10 cherry tomatoes, halved

2 tablespoons olive oil

1 small red onion, diced

½ teaspoon dried thyme

1 cup (250 ml) dry white wine or vegetable broth

Salt and pepper, to taste

1. Snip off the ends of the beans and remove the "string" that runs the length of the bean if it reveals itself. Rinse the beans under cold water, and put them in the slow cooker. Add the cherry tomatoes.

2. In a small skillet over medium-high heat, and add the oil and onion. Cook until the onion is just translucent, about 2 minutes. Remove from the heat and stir in the thyme. Put over beans in the slow cooker.

3. Add the white wine or vegetable broth. Cover and cook on Low for 2 to 3 hours. Season with the salt and pepper.

roasted root vegetables

If you like to shop farmers markets in the winter, you can often find a nice variety of root vegetables. Feel free to mix and match to your taste. Butternut squash is a great veggie to add to the mix, too.

makes 4 to 6 servings

1 large turnip, peeled and cubed

1 large parsnip, peeled and cubed

1 large potato, peeled and cubed

1 medium butternut squash, peeled, seeds removed, and cut into cubes

1 sweet onion, cut into thin wedges

6 cloves garlic, sliced thin

½ cup (120 ml) extra-virgin olive oil

Salt and pepper, to taste

1. In a large bowl, combine the cubed turnip, parsnip, potato, and squash, the onion wedges, and the sliced garlic.

2. Put everything into the slow cooker. Cover with the olive oil, and sprinkle with salt and pepper.

3. Cover and cook on Low for 5 to 6 hours, or on High for 3 to 4 hours, until vegetables are soft and fragrant.

4. Season with the salt and pepper and serve.

For a simple and straightforward variation, substitute a large sweet potato or three or four carrots for the butternut squash.

butternut squash and lentils

A fabulous fall stew that's loaded with vitamins from the squash and lentils.

makes 4 to 6 servings

3 large stalks celery, cut into ¼-inch (6 mm) thick slices

1 large white onion, chopped

1 large butternut squash, peeled, seeded, and cut into 1-inch (2.5 cm) chunks

1 16-ounce (460 g) bag brown lentils

4 cups (1 L) water

14 or 14.5-ounce (420 or 450 ml) can vegetable broth

½ teaspoon dried rosemary

¾ teaspoon salt

Parmesan cheese

¼ cup (15 g) loosely packed fresh parsley leaves, chopped

Salt and pepper, to taste

1. In slow cooker combine celery, onion, squash, lentils, water, broth, rosemary, and salt. Cover and cook on Low for 7 to 8 hours or on High for 4 to 6 hours, or until vegetables are tender.

2. Serve with Parmesan cheese and chopped parsley. Season with the salt and pepper if desired.

main dishes with meat

beef short ribs with rosemary and fennel

Short ribs are a wonderful cut because they become so meltingly tender when slowly braised in the slow cooker. The aromatic rosemary in the simple sauce cuts through the richness of the meat well.

makes 4 to 6 servings

Meaty short ribs with bones
(5 pounds, or 2.3 kg)

¼ cup (60 ml) olive oil

1 large onion, minced

2 cups (475 ml) beef
stock or broth

1 large fennel bulb, cored,
trimmed, and sliced

2 tablespoons fresh
parsley, chopped

2 tablespoons fresh rosemary

1 teaspoon cornstarch

Salt and pepper, to taste

1. Preheat the oven broiler, and line a broiler pan with heavy-duty aluminum foil. Broil short ribs for 3 to 4 minutes per side, or until browned. Arrange short ribs in the slow cooker, and pour in any juices that have collected in the pan.

2. Heat oil in a medium skillet over medium-high heat. Add onion and cook, stirring frequently, for 3 minutes, or until onion is translucent. Scrape mixture into the slow cooker. Add stock, fennel, parsley, and rosemary to the slow cooker, and stir well.

3. Cook on Low for 8 to 10 hours or on High for 4 to 5 hours, or until short ribs are very tender. Remove as much grease as possible from the slow cooker with a soup ladle.

4. If cooking on Low, raise the heat to High. Combine cornstarch with 2 tablespoons cold water in a small cup. Stir this mixture into the cooker, and cook on High for 15 to 20 minutes, or until juices are bubbling and slightly thickened. Season with the salt and pepper.

Including some simple vegetables adds texture and flavor to this dish. A half-pound (226 grams) of brussel sprouts (halved) and 3 or 4 fresh carrots (chopped or sliced) make an excellent addition to this hearty meal.

boeuf bourguignon

Simple, elegant, and classic French "stew" is the perfect meal to make for special occasions. It's irresistible.

makes 4 to 6 servings

Stewing beef (2 pounds, or 1 kg), fat trimmed, and cut into cubes

2 tablespoons olive oil

1 large onion, diced

3 cloves garlic, minced

½ pound (227 g) white mushrooms, rinsed, stemmed, and sliced thick

1½ cups (370 ml) dry red wine

1 cup (250 ml) beef stock (use real stock for this; it adds a whole other dimension)

1 tablespoon tomato paste

3 tablespoons fresh parsley, chopped

1 bay leaf

1 teaspoon herbes de Provence

1½ tablespoons arrowroot

Salt and pepper, to taste

1. Preheat the oven broiler, and line a broiler pan with heavy-duty aluminum foil. Broil beef cubes for 3 minutes per side, or until browned. Transfer cubes to the slow cooker, and pour in any juices that have collected in the pan.

2. Heat oil in a medium skillet over medium-high heat. Add onion, garlic, and mushrooms, and cook, stirring frequently, for 4 to 5 minutes, or until onion is translucent and mushrooms are soft. Scrape mixture into the slow cooker.

3. Add wine, stock, tomato paste, herbes de Provence, parsley, and a bay leaf to the slow cooker, and stir well. Cook on Low for 8 to 10 hours or on High for 4 to 5 hours, or until beef is very tender.

4. If cooking on Low, raise the heat to High. Combine arrowroot with 2 tablespoons cold water in a small cup, and stir it into the slow cooker. Cook on High for 15 to 20 minutes, or until juices are bubbling and slightly thickened. Remove and discard bay leaf, and season to taste with the salt and pepper. Garnish with some additional parsley if desired.

sweet-and-savory ham

The whole family will love what the combination of the sweet-and-savory flavors do to the ham during slow cooking. Be sure you're using a large slow cooker for this recipe.

makes 10 to 12 servings

Nonstick cooking spray

1 cooked spiral-sliced ham (6 to 8 pounds, or 2.8 kg to 3.8 kg)

1 8-ounce (227 g) can crushed pineapple

½ cup (120 ml) honey

¼ cup (32 g) firmly packed brown sugar

¼ cup (32 g) Dijon mustard

1. Spray the bottom of the slow cooker generously with the nonstick cooking spray.

2. Place the ham flat side down in the slow cooker. Pour the pineapple over the ham.

3. In a bowl, combine the honey, brown sugar, and mustard, and stir to thoroughly combine. Pour the sauce over the ham.

4. Cover and cook on Low for 6 to 8 hours or on High for 3 to 4 hours, finishing with a final 30 to 60 minutes on Low.

The history of the pineapple in America reveals why a pineapple-studded ham became a centerpiece of a holiday meal. Colonialists socialized quite a bit, and the ladies of the houses put together special centerpieces of fruit and vegetables on their dining room tables as a show of their wealth and status. The pineapple was the most special fruit one could include, and it was a must for any kind of special occasion.

zesty italian sausage and peppers

If you're looking for a super-simple dinner that will please the whole family, this is it. Serve the cooked sausages and sauce on thick hoagie rolls with a salad on the side, and everyone's happy.

makes 4 to 8 servings ~~~~~~

8 links sweet Italian sausage

1 24-ounce (680 g) jar of marinara sauce

1 clove garlic, minced

1 small Vidalia onion, sliced thin

1 large green bell pepper, cored, seeded, and cut into strips

8 hoagie rolls

1. Put all ingredients except the rolls in the slow cooker, and stir gently just to coat the meat and vegetables with the sauce.

2. Cook on Low for 6 to 8 hours. Serve on the rolls with the sauce.

For a spicier version, add half sweet sausage and half hot Italian sausage, and add a dash or two of red pepper flakes, and just a splash of Italian red wine!

herbed pork roast

Pork is a best friend of garlic, and this recipe calls for plenty of it! Between that and the fresh herbs, by the time this dish is cooked, everyone's mouths will be watering from the aroma.

makes 6 to 8 servings

1 boneless pork roast
(2 pounds, or 1 kg)

6 cloves garlic, minced

¼ cup (32 g) fresh
rosemary, chopped

2 tablespoons fresh
parsley, chopped

2 tablespoons fresh
sage, chopped

Salt and pepper, to taste

3 ribs celery, cut into
4-inch (10 cm) lengths

⅓ cup (80 ml) chicken
stock or broth

1. Rinse pork and pat dry with paper towels. Combine garlic, rosemary, parsley, sage, and season with the salt and pepper in a mixing bowl. Make slits deep in the pork, and stuff half of mixture into the slits. Rub remaining mixture on the outside of the roast.

2. Arrange celery slices in the bottom of the slow cooker to form a bed for the meat.

3. Preheat the oven broiler, and line a broiler pan with heavy-duty aluminum foil. Broil pork for 3 minutes per side, until well browned. Transfer pork to the slow cooker, and pour in any juices that have collected in the pan. Pour stock over pork.

4. Cover and cook on High for about 2 hours, then reduce heat to Low and cook for 4 hours, until pork is fork tender. Carve pork into slices and moisten with juices from the slow cooker.

Browning meat under the broiler accomplishes two things when using a slow cooker. It gives the meat a more appealing color, and it heats it so that it passes through the "danger zone" of 40°F to 140°F (4°C to 60°C) faster, especially if you're cooking on Low.

leg of lamb

While a slow-cooked lamb doesn't have the crunchy exterior of one roasted in the oven, it does produce a succulent roast. I am a fan of mint and mint jelly with lamb, but if you or your dinner companions aren't, just leave out the mint.

makes 4 to 6 servings

1 boneless leg of lamb (3 to 4 pounds or 1.4 kg to 1.8 kg)

1 tablespoon olive oil

½ teaspoon sea salt

½ teaspoon freshly ground black pepper

1 teaspoon fresh rosemary, chopped

1 teaspoon fresh mint, chopped (optional)

3 cloves garlic, minced

1. Put the olive oil in your hands and rub the oil all over the lamb.

2. Put the lamb in the slow cooker and sprinkle it all over with the salt, pepper, rosemary, mint, and garlic, rubbing the spices onto the meat.

3. Cover and cook on Low for 6 to 8 hours. Do not cook on High.

4. Season with additional salt and pepper if desired.

Serve with a delicious mint sauce or a mint jelly to take this oh-so-easy meal over the top. Both are available in specialty food stores.

duck a l'orange

Make this sweet-savory concoction in the slow cooker, and when the breasts are nice and tender, finish them under the broiler for a bit of crispiness that especially complements the sauce.

makes 2 to 4 servings

2 whole duck breasts (about 8 ounces, or 230 g) each, halved and skin removed

¼ cup (55 g) bacon or duck fat (or olive oil)

½ teaspoon salt

¼ teaspoon pepper

2 small oranges, peeled, seeded, and segments halved

1 Granny Smith or Empire apple, cored and cubed

1 onion, cut into small wedges

1 6-ounce can (178 ml) frozen orange juice concentrate, thawed

Nonstick cooking spray

1. Heat fat in slow cooker on Low. Add duck breasts, flesh side down. Sprinkle with salt and pepper. Add orange segments, apple, onion, and orange juice concentrate.

2. Cover and cook on Low for 6 to 8 hours, checking the meat to be sure it isn't overcooked, but that it is tender.

3. When almost ready to serve, preheat the broiler in the oven to high. Line a cookie sheet with foil and spray with nonstick cooking spray.

4. Place the breasts on the sheet. When the broiler is ready, put the cookie sheet in the oven. Broil about 4 minutes per side.

5. Remove solids from orange sauce and put sauce in a pitcher to serve on the side. Season with additional salt and pepper to taste.

Make a delicious ginger glaze for the meat, if desired. In a small saucepan, combine 1 tablespoon freshly grated ginger, 1 tablespoon fresh cilantro, chopped, 2 tablespoons honey, and about ½ cup (120 ml) water. Stir and bring to a boil, then remove from heat. Pour onto the meat or serve on the side.

simply sensational roast chicken

The slow cooking yields tender, fragrant meat. If you want crisp skin, put the cooked chicken under the broiler in the oven for about 5 minutes. Chances are it won't matter to you when this is done.

makes 4 to 6 servings

1 whole chicken (4 to 5 pounds, or 1.8 kg to 2.3 kg)

1 onion, cut into thick slivers

1 carrot, sliced

1 lemon

1 teaspoon dried thyme

1 teaspoon dried sage

1 teaspoon sea salt

1 teaspoon freshly ground black pepper

Parsley, for garnish

1. Place the slivers of onion and the sliced carrot in the slow cooker. Put the chicken on top of the vegetables. Squeeze the lemon over everything, then slice it into rounds and put a couple of the slices in the cavity of the bird. Season all over with thyme, sage, salt, and pepper.

2. Cover and cook on Low for 6 to 8 hours or on High for 3 to 4 hours. Season with additional salt and pepper, and chopped fresh parsley if desired.

You could substitute an already-made blend of spices called Poultry Seasoning for the thyme and sage. The poultry blend contains those herbs, as well as marjoram, parsley, and sometimes savory and rosemary.

tandoori chicken

I am a huge fan of the spices in this dish. While tandoori is typically done with a dry finish, this makes a succulent and juicy dish. Serve over cauliflower rice with a salad of fresh greens on the side.

makes 4 to 6 servings

1½ cups (360 ml) nonfat plain Greek yogurt

Juice from ½ lemon

½ teaspoon ground ginger

1 teaspoon ground cumin

1 teaspoon ground coriander

½ teaspoon paprika (sweet)

1 teaspoon turmeric

1 teaspoon salt

½ teaspoon cayenne pepper

Chicken pieces (4 pounds, or 1.8 kg) bones in, skin removed

1. In a bowl, combine the yogurt, and lemon juice. In another small bowl, combine the ginger, cumin, coriander, paprika, turmeric, salt, and cayenne pepper. Whisk the spices to combine well.

2. Add to the yogurt mix and stir to combine thoroughly.

3. Put the chicken pieces in a shallow baking dish and cover with the yogurt/spice mix. Cover the dish with plastic wrap and put it in the refrigerator. Allow to marinate overnight, or at least 8 hours.

4. Put the marinated chicken and the sauce in the slow cooker.

5. Cover and cook on Low for 8 to 10 hours, or on High for 4 to 6 hours, until the chicken is cooked through.

There is a lively and ongoing debate about whether yogurt is acceptable on a low-carb diet. In the research I've done, 8 ounces (227 g) of nonfat Greek yogurt has 8 grams of carbohydrates, so this dish calls for about 12 grams overall. There are so many nutritional benefits of Greek yogurt. It's a great treat in many ways.

chicken parmesan

If you're looking to make a low-carb version of chicken Parmesan, this recipe is done without breading the chicken first. It's easier to make and just as tasty (in my opinion). Serve with a large salad for a delicious meal.

makes 4 servings

4 boneless, skinless chicken breasts

2 teaspoons garlic powder

1 teaspoon salt

½ teaspoon pepper

1 tablespoon Italian seasoning mix

½ cup (80 g) Parmesan cheese, grated

1½ cups prepared marinara sauce (one with no added sugar is best)

8 ounces (230 g) shredded mozzarella cheese

1. Place the chicken breasts in the slow cooker. Season by sprinkling over them the garlic powder, salt, pepper, Italian seasoning, and a generous shaking of Parmesan cheese. Pour the mainara sauce over the meat.

2. Cover and cook on Low for 6 hours or on High for 4 hours.

3. Uncover and top the chicken with the mozzarella cheese, cover and cook on Low for another 30 minutes.

Rather than sprinkle the meat with the seasonings, you can add them to your spaghetti sauce before pouring it on the chicken. You can also try a marinara sauce that has basil or red peppers, so long as there is no sugar added.

indonesian chicken curry

If you're a fan of the bright smells and tastes of sesame, ginger, and coconut, you will love making this dish. It will perfume your kitchen and make your mouth water.

makes 4 to 6 servings

1½ pounds (680 g) boneless, skinless chicken breasts

1 tablespoon Asian sesame oil

2 tablespoons grated fresh ginger

3 scallions, white parts and 4 inches (10 cm) of green tops, chopped

3 cloves garlic, minced

2 tablespoons curry powder

1 teaspoon ground cumin

½ red bell pepper, seeds and ribs removed, cut into 1-inch (25 cm) squares

1 cup (250 ml) chicken broth or stock

1 cup (250 ml) coconut milk

2 tablespoons rice wine vinegar

1 tablespoon raw honey

1 cup (240 g) bok choy, sliced

2 ripe plum tomatoes, cored, seeded, and cut into sixths

2 tablespoons arrowroot

Salt and pepper, to taste

1. Rinse chicken and pat dry with paper towels. Cut chicken into 1-inch (2.5 cm) cubes.

2. Melt oil in a skillet over medium-high heat. Add ginger, scallions, and garlic, and cook, stirring frequently, for 30 seconds, or until fragrant. Reduce the heat to Low, and stir in curry powder and cumin. Cook for 1 minute, stirring constantly. Scrape mixture into slow cooker.

3. Add chicken, red bell pepper, stock, coconut milk, vinegar, and honey to the slow cooker, and stir well.

4. Cook on Low for 3 to 5 hours or on High for about 2 hours, or until chicken is cooked through.

5. Add bok choy and tomatoes, and cook for 1 more hour on Low or 30 minutes on High, or until bok choy is crisp-tender.

6. If cooking on Low, raise the heat to High. Combine arrowroot with 2 tablespoons cold water in a small cup. Stir mixture into the slow cooker, and cook for an additional 15 to 20 minutes, or until the liquid is bubbling and has slightly thickened. Season with the salt and pepper.

turkey breast

You might find yourself preparing this at the beginning of every week so you can slice into it as your week gets busy. It makes a lovely, finished meat that can be used to top salads, roll in lettuce leaves, or even eat out of the fridge.

makes 4 to 6 servings ~~~~~~

Boneless, skinless turkey breasts (4 pounds, or 1.8 kg)

½ teaspoon salt

¼ teaspoon pepper

1 tablespoon fresh rosemary, chopped

1 tablespoon fresh parsley, chopped

½ cup (120 ml) chicken stock or broth

1. Place the turkey in the slow cooker.

2. Sprinkle with salt and pepper. Add the herbs and stock.

3. Cover and cook on Low for 7 to 9 hours or on High for 4 to 6 hours, or until the meat is cooked through.

For easy-to-make, healthy, and delicious snacks, put cut cooked turkey onto a romaine lettuce leaf, and top with avocado slices, tomato slices, slivered almonds, and diced red onion. Roll the filling up in the leaf and enjoy.

chicken cacciatore

Cacciatore is Italian for "hunter's style," and since Italians in all regions are hunters, this dish is almost a national one. Though several meats can be featured in a cacciatore, they all include tomatoes, onions, pancetta, and mushrooms.

makes 4 to 6 servings

6 chicken pieces, thighs and legs or just thighs, skin removed

¼ cup (60 ml) olive oil

2 large onions, halved and thinly sliced

2 cloves garlic, minced

1 pound (454 g) cremini mushrooms, wiped with a damp paper towel, trimmed, and sliced

1 28-ounce (794 g) can diced tomatoes, undrained

½ cup (120 ml) dry white wine

1 tablespoon fresh thyme

1 tablespoon fresh sage, chopped

1 tablespoon fresh rosemary, chopped

Salt and pepper, to taste

1. Rinse chicken and pat dry with paper towels. Preheat the oven broiler, and line a broiler pan with heavy-duty aluminum foil. Broil chicken pieces for 3 minutes per side, or until browned. Transfer pieces to the slow cooker.

2. Heat oil in a large skillet over medium-high heat. Add onions, garlic, and mushrooms and cook, stirring frequently, for 5 minutes, or until mushrooms begin to soften. Scrape mixture nto the slow cooker.

3. Add tomatoes, wine, thyme, sage, and rosemary to the cooker, and stir well. Cook on Low for 6 to 8 hours or on High for 3 to 4 hours, or until chicken is cooked through, tender, and no longer pink.

4. Season with the salt and pepper.

Most of the mushrooms we find in supermarkets are the same species, "Agaricus bisporus." What makes the difference is their age. White button mushrooms are the youngest, cremini are in the middle, and portobello is what we call them when they're big and old.

arroz con pollo

This variation on a traditional Spanish-style chicken and rice has lots of peppers to add color and flavor.

Chicken pieces, preferably drumsticks and thighs (3 to 4 pounds, or 1.3 to 1.8 kg), skin removed

½ cup (60 ml) olive oil, divided

1 large white onion, diced

2 cloves garlic, minced

1 green bell pepper, seeds and ribs removed, diced

1 red bell pepper, seeds and ribs removed, and diced

1 teaspoon paprika

1 teaspoon ground cumin

2 teaspoons dried oregano

2 cups (500 ml) chicken broth

1 bay leaf

1 cup (195 g) uncooked converted long-grain rice

1 10-ounce (283 g) bag frozen peas

Salt, to taste

1. Preheat the oven broiler. Line a broiler pan with heavy-duty aluminum foil. Broil the chicken pieces for about 3 minutes on each side, until browned.

2. Heat 2 tablespoons of the oil in a medium skillet over medium-high heat. Add onion, garlic, and green and red bell peppers, and cook, stirring, until onion is translucent, about 4 minutes. Reduce the heat to low, add the paprika, cumin, and oregano, and cook for another minute or so, stirring constantly. Scrape mixture into the slow cooker.

3. Add chicken broth and bay leaf and stir well. Cover and cook on Low for 4 to 6 hours, or on High for 2 to 3 hours, until chicken is nearly cooked through.

4. While chicken is cooking, add the remaining 2 tablespoons of oil to the skillet. Add the rice and stir, cooking for 3 to 4 minutes, until grains are opaque and lightly browned. Remove the pan from the heat and set aside.

5. If cooking on Low, raise the heat to High. Add the rice to the slow cooker and cook another hour until the rice is almost tender and chicken is cooked through and tender. Add the peas and cook another 10 to 15 minutes.

6. Remove and discard bay leaf, season with salt, and serve.

spinach-stuffed turkey breast

This is a colorful dish, with a layer of bright green spinach and tasty prosciutto creating a spiral through the turkey.

1 boneless, skinless turkey breast half (2 pounds, or 1 kg)

1 10-ounce (283 g) package frozen chopped spinach, thawed

3 tablespoons low-fat milk

1 large egg

½ cup (64 g) panko bread crumbs

¼ pound (120 g) prosciutto

2 cloves garlic, cut into 4 slivers each

2 cups (500 ml) chicken broth

1 small white onion, sliced

1 carrot, peeled and sliced

4 sprigs fresh parsley

2 springs fresh thyme

1 bay leaf

1. Place turkey breast between two sheets of plastic wrap. Pound with the flat side of a meat mallet or the bottom of a small saucepan until it is a uniform thickness.

2. Place spinach in a colander and press with the back of a spoon to extract as much liquid as possible. Combine milk, egg, and bread crumbs in a mixing bowl, and whisk well. Stir in spinach.

3. Layer the prosciutto on top of the turkey breast, and spread spinach mixture on top. Roll turkey breast into a shape that will fit into your slow cooker, and tie with kitchen string. Make 8 slits in the meat and insert slivers of garlic into them.

4. Place the turkey breast in the slow cooker, and add broth, onion, carrot, parsley, thyme, and bay leaf. Cover and cook on Low for 6 to 8 hours or on High for 3 to 4 hours, or until turkey is cooked through and juices run clear.

5. Remove turkey from the slow cooker and transfer to a platter. Cut and discard string. Remove and discard the bay leaf from the sauce. Thinly slice the turkey, and pour some sauce over the entire portion.

thai chicken

Coconut milk, basil, and fish sauce combine to make a most fragrant and flavorful dish. A bowl of steaming rice noodles is the perfect accompaniment.

1 boneless, skinless chicken-breast halves, (1 pound, or 454 g)

3 tablespoons fish sauce

½ cup (120 ml) unsweetened coconut milk

1 tablespoon low-sodium soy sauce

1 tablespoon brown sugar

2 teaspoons canola oil

2 teaspoons fresh ginger, peeled and minced

1 clove garlic, crushed with a garlic press

1½ cups (60 g) loosely packed fresh basil leaves, coarsely chopped

1. Using a sharp knife, cut the chicken breast halves into ¼-inch (6 mm) slices. In a medium bowl, combine fish sauce, coconut milk, soy sauce, and brown sugar. Stir to combine thoroughly.

2. Put the chicken slices into the slow cooker, and top with the fish sauce mixture.

3. In a skillet over medium-high heat, add the oil and cook the ginger and garlic, stirring frequently, for about 2 minutes, until fragrant. Add to the slow cooker.

4. Top with the basil leaves, and stir all ingredients. Cover and cook on Low 5 to 6 hours or on High 3 to 4 hours, until chicken is cooked through.

For a slightly spicier version of this dish, add 1 tablespoon of fresh ground curry and two or three chopped red chili peppers. Zesty fun!

fish and seafood dishes

spicy shrimp scampi

This is a flavorful primi that is incredibly easy to make and always a hit. It's redolent with garlic, spicy from crushed red pepper, and brightly colored from a combination of paprika and parsley.

makes 6 to 8 servings

½ cup (120 ml) olive oil

6 garlic cloves, minced

1 tablespoon paprika

2 pounds (1 kg) extra-large shrimp, peeled and deveined

½ cup (120 ml) dry white wine

3 tablespoons fresh parsley, chopped

Salt and crushed red pepper flakes, to taste

Lemon wedges, for serving

1. Combine olive oil, garlic, paprika, shrimp, wine, and parsley in the slow cooker. Cook on Low for 3 to 4 hours or on High for 1½ to 2 hours, or until shrimp are pink and cooked through. Season to taste with salt and red pepper flakes.

2. Serve warm or at room temperature, and pass lemon wedges separately.

NOTE: The dish can be prepared up to a day in advance and refrigerated, tightly covered with plastic wrap. Allow it to sit at room temperature for 30 minutes before serving.

When you buy shrimp that are still in their shells, they need to be peeled, and that's an obvious task. Step two is to devein them. In one hand, hold the shrimp with its back facing up. With the other hand, cut gently down the back with a small paring knife. If there is a thin black line, scrape it out. That's the "vein"—it's actually the intestinal tract—which can be bitter and gritty.

white fish with lots of lemon

This is a recipe that takes full advantage of what's both fresh and possibly on sale in the seafood section of the store. All you need is fresh citrus and parsley to make a great meal.

makes 4 servings

Nonstick cooking spray

1½ pounds (680 g) fish fillets (use white-fleshed fish, like tilapia, flounder, cod, or haddock)

Salt and pepper, to taste

1 medium white onion, chopped

2 teaspoons lemon zest (finely grated rind)

2 teaspoons orange zest (finely grated rind)

¼ cup (60 ml) fresh-squeezed lemon juice

4 teaspoons olive oil

5 tablespoons parsley, chopped

1. Spray the slow cooker liberally with nonstick cooking spray. Season the fillets with the salt and pepper, and place fish in the slow cooker. Add the onion, zests, lemon juice, and oil.

2. Cover and cook on Low for 2 to 3 hours. Stir in the parsley.

catfish gumbo

This is a variation on a traditional gumbo, but it doesn't feature tomatoes. If you'd like, you can add a can of diced tomatoes (drained). Either way, the dish tastes good and is good for you!

makes 4 servings

Nonstick cooking spray

2 tablespoons olive oil

1 small white onion, chopped

1 clove garlic, minced

2 red bell peppers, seeded and cut into thin strips

1½ pounds (680 g) okra, trimmed, and sliced into ½-inch (12 mm) rounds

1 teaspoon lemon zest

Salt, to taste

1 cup (250 ml) water

4 5-ounce (140 g) catfish fillets

2 tablespoons fresh parsley, chopped

1. Spray the slow cooker with nonstick cooking spray.

2. In a large skillet, heat the oil over medium-high heat, add the onion and garlic, and cook, stirring, for about 3 minutes or until onion is translucent. Add the red bell pepper strips and continue stirring for another minute.

3. Put mixture into slow cooker, add okra, zest, and salt to taste. Stir to combine, then top with water.

4. Cover and cook on Low for 5 to 6 hours or on High for 3 to 4 hours until vegetables are tender.

5. Reduce or keep heat to Low and add the fish fillets. Cover and cook an additional 1 to 2 hours or until fish is cooked through and tender. Serve sprinkled with fresh parsley.

fennel, potato, and mussel melange

This dish is a hearty stew in which the mussels add their characteristic meaty succulence. With a salad of fresh greens on the side, it makes a delightful dish.

makes 4 servings

4 cups (1 L) low-sodium chicken broth, divided

⅔ teaspoon saffron

¾ cup (180 ml) olive oil

1 medium white onion, chopped

1 garlic clove, minced

1 small fennel bulb, fronds removed, washed and cored, then chopped

3 Idaho potatoes, peeled and diced

3 pounds (1.3 kg) mussels, scrubbed and beards removed

Sourdough bread

1 tablespoon fresh parsley, chopped

1. Pour 1 cup (250 ml) of the broth into a small bowl and add the saffron. Set aside. Cover the bowl with plastic wrap and refrigerate.

2. Warm oil in a skillet over medium heat, and add onion and garlic. Cook, stirring, for about 3 minutes or until onions are translucent.

3. Put the onion mixture into the slow cooker, and add the fennel, potatoes, and the remaining 3 cups (750 ml) of chicken broth.

4. Cover and cook on Low for 3 to 4 hours or on High for about 2 hours, or until vegetables are tender. If cooking on Low, turn heat to High. Add saffron broth and mussels, cover, and cook an additional 30 to 50 minutes, until mussels are open.

5. Serve in bowls with pieces of hearty sourdough bread. Garnish liberally with parsley.

clam sauce for spaghetti

The recipe calls for canned clams, which are the heart of the sauce, but adding fresh clams or mussels will make it extra special and delicious.

makes 4 servings

2 4-ounce (113 g) cans clams

1 pound (454 g) littleneck clams, scrubbed clean, if desired

1 8-ounce (236 ml) bottle clam juice

2 tablespoons olive oil

1 garlic clove, minced

1 teaspoon fresh ginger, grated

½ teaspoon lemon zest

Salt, to taste

1 pound (454 g) spaghetti or linguine

2 tablespoons fresh parsley

1. In a large bowl, combine clams, clam juice, olive oil, garlic, ginger, and zest. Stir well. Add salt to taste.

2. Put in slow cooker, cover, and cook on Low for 4 to 5 hours or on High for 3 to 4 hours, until clams open, indicating they are cooked.

3. Serve over bowls of spaghetti or linguine, and garnish with fresh parsley.

tilapia with aioli

Tilapia is a mild, white meat fish, which is the kind you want for this recipe. The aioli is a homemade garlicy mayonnaise-type sauce that makes a dish that melts in your mouth.

makes 2 to 4 servings

1 pound (454 g) tilapia fillets

2 cloves garlic

1 egg

¼ teaspoon salt

2 tablespoons lemon juice

½ cup (120 ml) olive oil

2 tablespoons Parmesan cheese

¼ cup (15 g) fresh parsley, chopped

1. Put tilapia fillets in the slow cooker.

2. Make the aioli. In a blender or food processor, put the garlic, egg, salt, and lemon juice. Blend on high for about 30 seconds until well combined. With the blender running on low, pour the olive oil in slowly.

3. The sauce will emulsify as you pour in the oil. Don't rush the process. When you've poured in all the oil and you have a thick sauce, turn off the blender. Pour the aioli over the fish. Sprinkle with Parmesan cheese.

4. Cover and cook on Low for about 2 to 3 hours, until the fillets are cooked through. Garnish with fresh parsley.

Tilapia is one of many varieties of fish in the cichlid family. They mainly inhabit freshwater ponds, streams, and lakes, and have been plentiful throughout time, with images of their capture in Egyptian hieroglyphics. Today the bulk of the tilapia in our stores comes from farm-raised fish, which is what keeps the price down.

tomato-braised tuna

Tuna is caught in the waters off Sicily, and in this recipe the gentle heat of the slow cooker glorifies this meaty fish while keeping it fairly rare. If you have any left over, you can add it to a mixed salad.

makes 4 to 6 servings

1 tuna steak in one thick slice (1½ to 2 pounds, or 680 g to 1 kg)

¼ cup (60 ml) olive oil, divided

½ small red onion, chopped

3 cloves garlic, minced

1 14.5-ounce (411 g) can diced tomatoes

1 teaspoon fresh basil, chopped

¼ teaspoon dried oregano

½ teaspoon dried rosemary

3 tablespoons capers, drained and rinsed

2 tablespoons fresh parsley, chopped

1 bay leaf

Salt and pepper, to taste

1. Soak tuna in cold water for 10 minutes. Pat dry with paper towels.

2. Heat 2 tablespoons of the oil in a large skillet over medium-high heat. Add onion and garlic and cook, stirring frequently, for 3 minutes, or until onion is translucent. Scrape mixture into the slow cooker. Add diced tomatoes, basil, dried herbs, capers, parsley, and bay leaf to the slow cooker and stir well. Cook on Low for 2 to 3 hours or on High for about 1 hour.

3. Heat remaining oil in the skillet over medium-high heat. Add tuna, and brown well on both sides. Add tuna to the slow cooker, and cook on Low for an additional 2 hours or on High for an additional hour or 90 minutes. Tuna should be cooked but still rare in the center. Remove and discard bay leaf, season with the salt and pepper, and serve hot.

Soaking the tuna in water removes a lot of its remaining blood, so that the finished dish is lighter in color and not bright red. The same treatment can be used on other dark fish, such as mackerel or bluefish.

fish kabobs

The nice thing about making kabobs in the slow cooker is that you don't have to worry about parts or all of them burning on the grill.

⅓ cup (80 ml) olive oil

1 tablespoon herbes de Provence

2 cloves garlic, mashed

¼ teaspoon salt

½ teaspoon pepper

2 pounds (1 kg) monkfish or salmon, cut into cubes

12 to 16 small Brussels sprouts, cleaned and tough bottoms cut off

1 onion, cut into thick wedges

1 large zucchini, cut into large slices

1 small package cherry tomatoes

Wooden skewers, cut or broken into sizes to fit into the slow cooker

1. In a large bowl, combine the olive oil, herbes de Provence, garlic, salt, and pepper, and stir to combine. Add the fish, Brussels sprouts, onions, and zucchini, and toss to coat all.

2. Put the fish and vegetables onto the skewers, working in the cherry tomatoes. Put the skewers in the slow cooker as you finish them. Pour the remaining dressing over the skewers.

3. Cook on Low for 3 to 4 hours or on High for 2 to 3 hours until fish is cooked through and vegetables are tender.

Spice this recipe up by adding some cayenne to the dressing, or by including slices of fresh seeded, sliced jalapenos or other hot peppers.

A side of sour cream with diced chives is also a nice addition to this dish.

salmon cakes

These are so easy to make! Serve with fresh lettuce, tomato, and thinly sliced red onions.

makes 4 servings

2 14.5-ounce (411 g) cans cooked salmon

¼ cup (25 g) oat bran

2 scallions, white parts only, minced fine

½ cup (75 g) red pepper, minced

½ teaspoon salt

1 teaspoon cayenne pepper

2 eggs

½ cup or 1 stick (120 g) unsalted butter, melted, divided

1 lemon, cut into wedges

1. Drain the salmon and empty the cans into a large bowl, flaking the meat. Add the oat bran, scallions, red pepper, salt, cayenne, and eggs, and stir to combine. Melt 6 tablespoons of the butter and add to the fish mix, stirring. Form the fish mix into 4 patties.

2. Melt 2 tablespoons of the butter in a skillet and brown the patties on both sides.

3. Transfer to the slow cooker. Cover and cook on Low for 3 to 4 hours until fish is cooked through, turning the cakes midway through. Serve hot with lemon wedges.

Vary the flavor by substituting 1 tablespoon of fresh dill, chopped fine, for the teaspoon of cayenne pepper.

hearty fish stew

Crayfish are one of the few mollusks that don't have carbohydrates. They are popular in Cajun cooking. Resembling mini lobsters, they turn bright red when they're cooked. Getting the flesh out of the shells is a culinary challenge. If they're not available in your area, just do without.

makes 4 to 6 servings

¾ pound (340 g) thick firm-fleshed fish fillets, such as cod, swordfish, or halibut

¼ pound (120 g) extra-large shrimp

1 dozen crayfish (optional)

3 tablespoons olive oil

2 medium onions, diced

1 red bell pepper, seeds and ribs removed, and finely chopped

2 celery ribs, diced

3 cloves garlic, minced

2 tablespoons fresh oregano, chopped

2 teaspoons fresh thyme

1 28-ounce (794 g) can diced tomatoes, undrained

2 tablespoons tomato paste

2 cups (480 ml) white wine

1 bay leaf

¼ cup (60 ml) fresh parsley, chopped

3 tablespoons fresh basil, chopped

Salt and pepper, to taste

1. Rinse fish and pat dry with paper towels. Remove and discard any skin or bones. Cut fish into 1-inch (2.5 cm) cubes.

2. Peel and devein the shrimp. Wash the crayfish thoroughly, if using. Refrigerate all seafood until ready to use, tightly covered with plastic wrap.

3. Heat oil in a medium skillet over medium-high heat. Add onions, red bell pepper, celery, garlic, oregano, and thyme. Cook, stirring frequently, for 3 minutes, or until onions are translucent. Scrape mixture into the slow cooker.

4. Add tomatoes, tomato paste, wine, and bay leaf to the slow cooker and stir well to dissolve tomato paste. Cook on Low for 5 to 7 hours or on High for 2 to 3 hours, until vegetables are almost tender.

5. If cooking on Low, raise the heat to High. Add seafood, parsley, and basil. Cook 1 hour or so, or until fish is cooked through. Remove and discard bay leaf, and season with the salt and pepper.

shrimp creole

The Creole cuisine of Louisiana is an amalgam of French, Italian, and Spanish influences tempered with African-American culture, and shrimp Creole is one of its premier dishes.

makes 4 to 6 servings

3 tablespoons olive oil

6 scallions, white parts and 3 inches of green tops, chopped

2 celery ribs, sliced

½ green bell pepper, seeded and diced

3 cloves garlic, minced

1 tablespoon dried oregano

1 tablespoon paprika

1 teaspoon ground cumin

½ teaspoon dried basil

1 15-ounce (425 g) can tomato sauce

½ cup (120 ml) white wine

2 bay leaves

1½ pounds (680 g) extra-large shrimp, peeled and deveined

Salt and cayenne pepper, to taste

1. Heat oil in a medium skillet over medium-high heat. Add scallions, celery, bell pepper, and garlic. Cook, stirring frequently, for 3 minutes, or until scallions are translucent.

2. Reduce the heat to low, and stir in oregano, paprika, cumin, and basil. Cook for about 1 minute, stirring constantly. Scrape mixture into the slow cooker.

3. Add tomato sauce, wine, and bay leaves to the slow cooker, and stir well. Cook on Low for 4 to 6 hours or on High for 2 to 3 hours, or until vegetables are soft.

4. If cooking on Low, raise the heat to High. Remove and discard bay leaves and stir in shrimp. Cook for 15 to 30 minutes, or until shrimp are pink and cooked through. Season to taste with salt and cayenne.

Do not equate the words "fresh shrimp" with shrimp that have never been frozen. The truth is you probably would be unable to find never-frozen shrimp fresh from the ocean unless you net it yourself. That's because these days shrimp are harvested, cleaned, and flash-frozen on the boats before they ever reach the shore. But if you plan to freeze shrimp, ask the fishmonger to sell you some still frozen rather than thawed in the case.

maryland crabs

You can pretend you're visiting the Chesapeake Bay area by making crabs seasoned with Old Bay. If you want to get authentic, cover your picnic table with brown paper and pile the crabs on top to eat. When you've picked through the shells, roll up the paper and toss the whole mess.

makes 4 servings

2 cups (500 ml) water

½ cup (120 ml) distilled vinegar

¼ cup (7 g) Old Bay Seasoning

1 tablespoon salt

6 to 8 blue crabs, about 1 pound (454 g) each

½ cup or 1 stick (60 g) unsalted butter, melted

1. In a bowl, combine the water, vinegar, seasoning, and salt until well combined. Pour into the slow cooker. Cover and turn to High. After 1 hour, add the crabs. Cover again and continue to cook on High for about 2 more hours, until crabs have turned bright red and cooked through.

2. Divide the butter into bowls for dipping.

It's so worth the splurge to order Maryland blue crabs online. They arrive super-fresh and ready to cook and eat. What a treat!

swordfish with ginger-maple balsamic

If you like a sweet-spicy flavor combo, this is a great dish. The ginger (spicy), balsamic (sour but slightly sweet), and maple (sweet but not cloying) seasonings bring the fish alive.

¼ cup (60 ml) olive oil

3 tablespoons lemon juice

2 cloves garlic, chopped

½ teaspoon salt

½ cup (120 ml) dry white wine

2 pounds (1 kg) swordfish steaks

½ cup (120 ml) balsamic vinegar

1 tablespoon maple syrup (all natural)

1 teaspoon fresh grated ginger

½ to 1 teaspoon cornstarch

1. In a bowl, combine the olive oil, lemon juice, garlic, salt, and wine. Pour into the slow cooker. Put the swordfish steaks in the cooker. Cover and cook on Low for 4 hours or until the fish is cooked through.

2. Make the sauce on the stove by combining the balsamic, syrup, and ginger in a small saucepan. Bring to a boil then reduce heat to a simmer. Cook until the sauce has been reduced and thickened, about 30 minutes, stirring regularly. If desired to thicken more, sprinkle a very small amount of cornstarch in it and whisk. Serve the sauce over the swordfish steaks.

This is also delicious with tuna steaks, or even with lobster tails or monkfish. The sweet-salt sauce calls for a firm or substantial piece of fish.

fish veracruz

People seem to lose sight of the fact that most of Mexico is surrounded by coastline because so much of our beloved Tex-Mex food is based on dishes from landlocked Sonora province. This delicate fish in a spicy sauce is wonderful on its own or in a lettuce wrap.

makes 4 to 6 servings

2 tablespoons olive oil

2 onions, thinly sliced

4 cloves garlic, minced

1 jalapeno or Serrano pepper, seeds and ribs removed, finely chopped (wear rubber gloves to do this)

1 tablespoon chili powder

2 teaspoons dried oregano

1 14.5-ounce (411 g) can diced tomatoes, drained

1 cup (240 ml) white wine

2 tablespoons freshly squeezed lemon juice

2 tablespoons tomato paste

1 teaspoon grated lemon zest

¼ cup (60 ml) black or green olives (packed in oil or water with no additional chemicals)

1½ pounds (680 g) cod or halibut, cut into serving pieces

Salt and pepper, to taste

1. Heat oil in a medium skillet over medium-high heat. Add onions, garlic, and pepper. Cook, stirring frequently, for 3 minutes, or until onion is translucent. Reduce the heat to low, and stir in chili powder and oregano. Cook for 1 minute, stirring constantly. Scrape mixture into the slow cooker.

2. Add tomatoes, wine, lemon juice, tomato paste, and lemon zest to the slow cooker, and stir well.

3. Cook for 4 to 6 hours on Low, or 2 to 3 hours on High, until vegetables are tender.

4. Add the fish pieces and stir gently. If cooking on Low, raise the heat to High and cook for an additional 25 to 35 minutes, or until fish is cooked through and flakes easily. Stir in the olives and allow to heat through. Season with the salt and pepper.

Chili powder is a premixed blend of herbs and spices. If you make it yourself, you can personalize the taste to suit your own. The base should be ground red chiles and ground cumin. Then add as much paprika, ground coriander, cayenne, and oregano as you like. Some brands also include garlic powder and some onion.

brook trout with lemon

This recipe calls for cooking the fish whole, but don't worry—filleting it when it's cooked is easy. It makes an elegant presentation on the plate, and there's something very satisfying about removing the skeleton yourself.

makes 2 to 4 servings

2 medium to large whole brook trout, cleaned by the fishmonger, but not filleted

2 lemons

2 teaspoons herbes de Provence

Salt, to taste

2 tablespoons salted butter

⅔ cup (160 ml) dry white wine

1 tablespoon fresh parsley, chopped

1. Put 1 trout each on pieces of aluminum foil that are big enough to wrap over the fish to form a sealed cooking "tent." With the trout in the middle of the piece of foil, squeeze the juice of 1 lemon over each, removing seeds as you go. Sprinkle each fish with a teaspoon of herbes de Provence and some salt. Cut the butter into 4 small pieces and place two pats each on top of the fish. If desired, slice the lemons and place 2 slices in the cavity inside each fish.

2. Bring up the sides of the foil and begin to form the packet. When the sides are up, pour ⅓ cup (80 ml) wine on each trout before securing all edges together and fully enclosing the fish.

3. Put the trout packets in the slow cooker. Cook on Low for 2 to 3 hours or on High for 1 to 2 hours. Half way through, peek into one of the packets to see how the fish is doing. It's cooked when the flesh is pale and easily flakes away from the bones. Make sure it's cooked through before removing from packets and serving. Serve whole, pouring the sauce in the packet over the fish. Garnish with parsley.

Removing the trout's skeleton so your fish is free of bones is easy if you take your time. With the fish on your plate, loosen the flesh close to the spine and gently scrape/slide the top "fillet" off the skeleton. When it's off and half the skeleton is exposed, lift the head or tail of the trout and gently pull back and lift up to pull the remaining skeleton away from the fillet on the bottom. Discard the skeleton.

delicious desserts

rice pudding

Once you master this simple recipe, you can add fruits and flavorings to the pudding. Its creamy goodness from low-fat ingredients makes it taste like it has more calories than it does.

makes 4 servings

Nonstick cooking spray

1 cup (185 g) Arborio rice

1 14-ounce (420 ml) can unsweetened coconut milk

1 13.5-ounce (400 ml) can low-fat condensed milk

2 cups (480 ml) low-fat milk

½ teaspoon cinnamon or nutmeg

Pinch salt

Fresh mint sprigs, if desired

1. Grease the inside of the slow cooker liberally with the nonstick spray. Combine rice, coconut milk, condensed milk, milk, cinnamon or nutmeg, and salt in the slow cooker. Stir well.

2. Cook on Low for 5 to 7 hours, or on High for 2 to 3 hours. Rice should be soft and the liquid thick when it is thoroughly cooked. Serve hot, warm, or chilled, and top with fresh sprigs of mint, if desired.

raspberry-pear cobbler

A cobbler is a simple dessert based on adding fruit to a basic cake recipe. The fruit is the star of the dessert, though, so pile it on!

makes 4 servings

1 cup (125 g) all-purpose flour

¾ cup (170 g) brown sugar, packed down

1 teaspoon baking powder

¼ teaspoon salt

¼ teaspoon ground cinnamon

¼ teaspoon ground nutmeg

2 eggs, lightly beaten

3 tablespoons vegetable oil

2 tablespoons low-fat milk

4 cups (440 g) fresh or frozen raspberries

2 cups (300 g) fresh or frozen Bosc pears, cored and cut into cubes

1 cup (240 ml) water

3 tablespoons quick-cooking tapioca

½ cup (170 g) maple syrup

1. In a medium bowl, stir together flour, brown sugar, baking powder, salt, cinnamon, and nutmeg. In a small bowl, combine eggs, oil, and milk. Add egg mixture all at once to flour mixture. Stir just until moistened. Set aside.

2. In a large saucepan, combine berries and pears, the water, and tapioca. Bring to a boil. Add maple syrup to hot fruit mixture, remove from heat, and put into the slow cooker. Immediately spoon the batter over the fruit mixture.

3. Cover and cook on Low for 4 to 5 hours or on High for 1 to 2 hours. Test for doneness by inserting a toothpick in the center. If it comes out clean, it's done. When done, turn the cooker off, leave uncovered, and let stand for about 30 minutes or an hour to cool. Serve warm.

baked pears with ginger

Use pears that are nice and ripe to get the most flavor from this aromatic and satisfying dish.

makes 4 servings

4 large, ripe Anjou or Bosc pears, cored and cut into chunks or slices

1 teaspoon ground ginger

1 teaspoon lemon zest

2 tablespoons butter, cut into bits

1. Put the pear slices into the slow cooker. Sprinkle with the ginger and the lemon zest. Put bits of butter over the fruit.

2. Cover and cook on Low for 3 to 4 hours or on High for about 2 hours. Serve warm or at room temperature.

Add some crunch to the recipe by topping with toasted nuts—pepitas, sesame seeds, and almonds are all good choices.

baked peaches

Ripe peaches are so juicy that, when slow-cooked, they make a summer slurry. Stir in some toasted nuts for added crunch when serving.

makes 4 servings

4 large, ripe peaches, peeled, pits removed, and cut into slices

1 teaspoon cinnamon

1 teaspoon lemon zest

2 tablespoons honey

1. Put the peach slices into the slow cooker. Sprinkle with the cinnamon and the lemon zest. Drizzle with honey.

2. Cover and cook on Low for 3 to 4 hours or on High for about 2 hours. Serve warm or at room temperature.

Turn the recipe into a crumble or crisp by adding a topping of ½ cup (55 g) almond flour mixed with 1 tablespoon coconut butter and some toasted almonds. Put the crumble on top of the fruit before cooking.

pumpkin custard

You can use canned organic pumpkin puree for this recipe, or you can use freshly baked or steamed pumpkin.

makes 6 to 8 servings

6 egg yolks

1¼ cups (300 ml) coconut milk

1 teaspoon pumpkin pie spice mix

½ cup (80 g) sugar

½ teaspoon vanilla extract

⅛ teaspoon salt

⅓ cup (90 g) pumpkin puree

½ toasted almond slices or pumkin seeds

1. Put an oven-safe casserole dishor several ceramic ramekins into the slow cooker. Add water around the dish(es) so that it reaches about halfway up the sides.

2. In a large bowl using a whisk, beat the egg yolks until thoroughly combined and a lighter, lemony color. Add the coconut milk, spice mix, sugar, vanilla, and salt and combine until well combined. Fold in the pumpkin puree. Pour the mixture into the dish inside the slow cooker.

3. Cover and cook on Low for 5 to 6 hours or on High for 2 to 4 hours. The custard should be thick but not too firm. Turn the cooker off and let the dish cool slightly in the water. Then remove it and refrigerate for an hour or longer before serving. Garnish with toasted almond slices or pumpkin seeds.

Pumpkin pie spice mix is a premade combination of cinnamon, ginger, nutmeg, and allspice. If you'd like to experiment with bringing out certain of these flavors, use them individually.

light-as-a-feather almond cake

This is a delicious, airy cake that contains no egg yolks. Cooked in the slow cooker, it won't necessarily be the most elegant dessert you've ever put on the table, but it might well be one that is eaten the fastest!

makes 4 to 6 servings

1¼ cups (155 g) almonds, shelled but with the peel

½ cup (170 g) honey

1 tablespoon lemon zest (no pith)

6 tablespoons almond flour

8 large eggs, separated

Pinch salt

1. Line the slow cooker with a large piece of parchment paper so that it comes up over the sides.

2. In a blender or food processer, grind the almonds to a fine consistency. Put them in a bowl and stir in the honey, lemon zest, and almond flour.

3. In a large bowl, beat the egg whites with the salt until they form stiff peaks. Fold the almond mixture into the egg whites.

4. Using a spatula, transfer the cake mixture into the slow cooker. Cover and cut away any excess parchment paper around the lid to ensure a tight fit. Cook on Low for 6 to 8 hours or on High for 4 to 6 hours. Test for doneness by inserting a toothpick in the center. If it comes out clean, it's done. The cake should be set on top. Remove with the parchment paper and invert onto a serving platter.

Topping this sunny dessert with sliced fruits will bring a taste of the tropics to your table.

fall fruit crisp

The fruits used to make this earthy dessert are available year-round in most places, so you can enjoy it any time of year.

makes 4 to 6 servings

3 cups (450 g) baking apples, like Northern Spy or Mutsu, peeled and thinly sliced

3 cups (450 g) Anjou or Bosc pears, cored and cubed

½ cup (75 g) dates, chopped

2 teaspoons fresh-squeezed lemon juice

1½ cups (150 g) toasted pecans, crumbled

½ cup (55 g) flour

½ teaspoon ground cinnamon

½ teaspoon ground ginger

¼ teaspoon ground nutmeg

½ cup (170 ml) maple syrup

¼ cup (55 g) unsalted butter

Vanilla ice cream

½ cup (110 g) roasted pepitas (pumpkin seeds) for garnish

4 to 8 fresh mint leaves, rinsed (optional)

1. In a large bowl, combine fruits, dates, and lemon juice. Combine well and transfer to the slow cooker.

2. In another bowl, combine the pecans, flour, spices, and maple syrup and stir to combine.

3. Using the tines of a fork or a pastry blender, work in the butter. Mixture will become a coarse "crumble." Sprinkle this evenly over the fruit mixture in the slow cooker.

4. Cover and cook on Low for 3 to 4 hours or on High for about 2 hours, or until fruit is tender. Serve warm or at room temperature. Top with ice cream and pepitas. Garnish with fresh mint, if desired.

Maple syrup is relatively low in fructose, and full of beneficial minerals, including potassium, manganese, iron, and calcium.

chocolate fondue

This is one of the desserts you can prepare in the slow cooker for short-notice occasions. It only needs about an hour of cooking time. While this is happening (and you don't need to stir), you can cut up things to dip into it, like bananas, apples, pound cake, pretzels, and other goodies.

makes 4 servings

¾ pound (340 g) good-quality bittersweet chocolate, chopped

½ cup (120 ml) heavy whipping cream

3 tablespoons liqueur or liquor or rum extract if you want a non-alcoholic fondue

1. Combine chocolate, cream, and liqueur or extract in the slow cooker. Cook on Low for 45 to 60 minutes, or until chocolate melts. Stir gently toward the end of the cooking time.

2. Serve directly from the slow cooker, using large toothpicks or fondue forks to dip the selection of foods.

The fondue can be flavored with any number of liqueurs or liquors, including rum, bourbon, tequila, brandy, triple sec, kirsch, crème de cacao, Irish Cream, raspberry liqueur, or even chocolate liqueur.

panettone bread pudding

Panettone is a sweet yeast bread that originated in Milan and is traditionally served at Christmas. It usually contains some sort of dried fruit as well as candied citrus peel.

3 large eggs

1 cup (200 g) sugar

1 ¾ cup (410 ml) whole milk

6 tablespoons (85 g) unsalted butter, melted

½ teaspoon vanilla extract

¼ teaspoon ground cinnamon

Pinch salt

5 cups (175 g) cubed panettone

¼ cup (40 g) golden raisins

½ cup (80 g) mixed candied fruits

Nonstick cooking spray

Whipped cream (optional)

1. Whisk eggs in a large mixing bowl with sugar until thick and lemon-colored. Whisk in milk, melted butter, vanilla, cinnamon, and salt. Add bread cubes, and press down with the back of a spoon so they absorb the egg mixture. Stir in raisins and candied fruit.

2. Spray the slow cooker liberally with the nonstick spray. Spoon the mixture into the slow cooker. Cook on High for 1 hour, then reduce heat to Low and cook for 2 to 3 hours, or until a toothpick inserted into the center comes out clean and an instant-read thermometer inserted into the center reads 165°F (74°C). Serve hot or at room temperature, with whipped cream if desired.

While Panettone is the bread traditionally used in Italy for bread puddings, it's sometimes hard to find other than at Christmas time in many supermarkets. You can always substitute challah, brioche, or other rich egg breads.

honey-kissed figs

This makes a Fig Newton—like substance that has all the freshness of the figs without the additives found in the highly processed cookie centers.

makes about 2 cups ～～～～～～～～～～～～～～～～～～～

2 pounds (1 kg) fresh figs, stems removed, peeled and cut into eighths

Juice from 1 lemon

½ cup (120 ml) water

½ cup (170 g) honey

Fresh whipped cream or vanilla ice cream

1. Put the peeled and cut figs in the slow cooker. Squeeze the lemon over the fruit, removing the seeds that come out. Combine the water and honey in a bowl and combine. Pour over the figs.

2. Cover and cook on Low for 6 to 8 hours or on High for 4 to 5 hours. Allow to cool before serving. Serve with whipped cream or ice cream.

Figs are actually one of the oldest known fruits, originating in northern Asia Minor—so it might have been the true treat of our Paleo ancestors. They were cooked to use as sweeteners long before the discovery of sugar. Figs are loaded with fiber, iron, and potassium.

lemon poppy seed cake

Dense and lemony, this is a great dessert to satisfy your sweet tooth and your tastebuds!

Nonstick cooking spray

½ cup (55 g) coconut flour

½ teaspoon salt

¼ teaspoon baking soda

6 eggs

½ cup (120 ml) vegetable oil

¼ cup (85 g) honey

1 teaspoon vanilla extract

Zest of 1 lemon

2 tablespoons fresh squeezed lemon juice

1½ tablespoons poppy seeds

Fresh strawberries, blueberries, raspberries, or a combination for garnish

1. Spray a bread loaf pan liberally with nonstick cooking spray and place inside the slow cooker. If it doesn't fit, line the slow cooker with aluminum foil, making sure the edges go up over the unit. Spray the aluminum foil with the nonstick cooking spray.

2. In a small bowl, combine the coconut flour, salt, and baking soda. Combine well and set aside.

3. In a large bowl, whisk the eggs until combined. Add the oil, honey, vanilla, lemon zest, and lemon juice and stir to combine. Mix in the flour mixture, and then stir in the poppy seeds.

4. Pour the batter into the loaf pan or foil-lined slow cooker. Cover and cook on Low for 7 to 9 hours or on High for 4 to 5 hours. Test for doneness by inserting a toothpick in the center. If it comes out clean, it's done.

5. When cooked, remove the loaf pan from the cooker or carefully lift out the foil. Allow to cool slightly, and then transfer to a serving dish. Garnish with fresh berries if desired.

This cake is delicious warm or chilled. For an even fruitier dessert, berries can be added to the batter before cooking. Use 1 cup (145 g) fresh berries and fold them into the batter just before transferring to the slow cooker. You may need to increase the cooking time slightly to accommodate the moisture of the fresh berries in the cooking process.

flan

No cook is without plenty of eggs on hand during the holidays. This classic custard recipe is another great way to use them to the delight of all who partake.

Nonstick cooking spray

½ cup (100 g) sugar

3 eggs

⅛ teaspoon salt

1½ cups (360 ml) whole milk

¾ teaspoon vanilla extract

1. Spray the insides of four 6-ounce (180 ml) ceramic ramekins and place in the slow cooker. Add water slowly and carefully to go around the ramekins so that it comes about halfway up the cups.

2. In a small skillet over medium heat, cook ¼ cup (50 ml) of the sugar until it melts into a light brown syrup, stirring constantly. Pour the syrup into the ramekins.

3. In a large bowl, combine eggs, salt, and remaining sugar. Beat with an electric mixer on low until the mixture is a pale lemon color. With mixer still on low, gradually beat in milk and vanilla extract. When combined, distribute the mixture among the ramekins.

4. Cover and cook on Low for about 8 hours or on High for about 4 hours. Custards should be set but not overcooked. Remove and allow to cool. When serving, slide a knife around the rim to loosen the custard, and invert onto a plate so that the sugar syrup runs down the sides.

For an added flavor boost, consider including 1 teaspoon lemon zest. Stir it in with the milk and vanilla toward the end of the instructions.